D0995506

WELLBEING

Alison Webster

scm press

British Library Cataloguing in Publication data

A catalogue record for this book is available from the British Library

Bible quotations are taken from
The New Revised Standard Version © 1989

0 334 028892

First published in 2002 by SCM Press
9-17 St Albans Place, London N1 0NX

www.scm-canterburypress.co.uk

SCM Press is a division of
SCM-Canterbury Press Ltd

Printed and bound in Great Britain by
Bookmarque, Croydon

For Ashley

CONTENTS

PREFACE

Society and Church

Why is there any need to commission books on society and Church? Is there anything really to discuss? That suspicious question may be asked from at least two quite diverse perspectives. On the one hand, most people in our highly secularized society will regard Church as, at most, an institution of voluntary association (like the Royal Society for the Protection of Birds or a Cycling association), attracting like-minded people. It may (or may not) be thought a good thing (for other people, who are into that sort of thing). Church is unlikely, however, to be considered essential to the fabric or self-understanding of society as a whole, even by those who admit Christianity's historically significant role in the self-understanding and development of our society and polity. Entirely marginal to society, like the RSPB and cycling groups, it may allowably engage with wider society in order to pursue its special interest agenda (protection of birds, provision of cycle lanes). But it would have to do so by arguing and campaigning on commonly agreed ground, not by appeal to some special sense of what society and social good are.

On the other hand, those within churches might feel there is little point in asking whether and how Church relates to society, since it is manifestly obvious that, empirically, it just does. Simply as a social institution existing within society, the Church is necessarily and unavoidably actively engaged in it theologically, spiritually, educationally, whilst, as institution, it has had to respond to its changing context. At one level, this is an empirical statement, yet it is one that will often receive a theological expression and interpretation. Social engagement is often seen, not as incidental, accidental or peripheral matters – what the Church *does* – but aspects of its central self-definition – what the Church *is.* The Church's institutional engagement in education, welfare, government, and so on, may be seen in terms of the Church's self-defining mission, or as part of its self-understanding. The ways in which Church is engaged in society reflects a long history in which, at its best, the Church has held a dynamic and historical vision of its task and existence, grounded in the mystery of the Trinitarian God. (In the last century the Church has abandoned a static view of ministry, and no longer sees itself as given its final form by Christ at its origin. Theologians and church members respond in many changing ways to the world around it.) The Church as an institution adapts to its changing circumstances, whilst also pronouncing on matters of societal concern within those areas historically within its remit.

Yet such a confident note belies the crisis which afflicts the very existence of the Church in British society. In the last fifty years culture has become almost completely secularized in its public sphere. The language of God, once quite common in public life in the first half of the twentieth century, and for centuries before that, is now muted, if not almost silent. The occasional politician refers to God in a half-embarrassed way, or religion is seen as dangerous, irrational and the cause of wars and terrorism. The Church and God-talk are marginalized. Moreover, where the Church does engage with society, on issues of social and political concern, it finds difficulty in seeing the possibility and significance of God-talk too. The Church tends to adopt secular modes of discernment and secular criteria in its reports and contributions to debate. In this situation it is far from clear how the rapid changes inside the churches in the last fifty years relate at all to the indifference of the world. How may the churches make any contribution to British society?

Asking this question is the task of this series. The purpose of *Society and Church* is to ask how the churches may claim public space, as *Christian* churches, in a legitimate and effective way in a society that has become as secular as British society now is. The question will be answered in a way that engages with three overlapping, but distinct audiences. First, there will be church people who care about the future of the Church and of society. Second, there are those who might be called the half-believer. They will read religious articles in the press, or will listen to religious programmes on radio and television, but are unlikely to enter a church building except occasionally: they believe and doubt (or believe but fail to find the relevance and significance of God – or at least Church) at the same time. Third, there are those suspicious of the Church, or not terribly interested in religion, but who are committed to the topic and will read the book for the sake of the subject.

The series will address the central issue of the marginalization of the Church by commissioning books on specific topics, in a concrete way that avoids abstraction. On this issue is there anything which is illuminated by referring to a theological standpoint, within the specific historical, cultural, political and ecclesiastical dynamics of the situation? The purpose of this approach is to see how the distinctiveness of what is modelled in one work may illuminate another quite different situation. 'I had not thought that you could look at it in this way.' The series will not share one particular way of reading the situation, nor hold a particular theological or political viewpoint. We shall commission from left and right (whatever those terms might mean in our postmodern world), but we will always emphasize that the relationship of Church and society has changed so much in the new millennium that conventional religious and theological strategies are no longer appropriate.

It is clear that this analysis is not shared widely inside the churches. There is rather a sense of complacency about the present and future status and contribution of the Church to national life in Britain. Equally there is no clear understanding among the churches either of what their relationship to society might be, or how it might be effectively defended. Theologically there is grave doubt as to whether public theology is possible any more. A public theology has theological integrity in addressing society, while being responsible to the issues in society. In Church terms, it means that the idea of being 'a Church for society' is deeply problematic.

Those who write in this series are those who take this crisis with the utmost seriousness. They believe that the Church still has something to offer society, and believe that it is part of its very rationale that it should do so, but who understand all too well the difficulties of the present time. The series will take into account the massive changes that have occurred in British society and politics since 1945, and authors will refer to these developments in their particular work. But the series is not an exercise in contemporary history. The aim of the series is to initiate a conversation as to whether public theology is any longer possible. Have the churches anything to say which it is worth the world listening to? That is the stark question addressed by this series.

Alison Webster writes at a time when our understanding of human health, wellbeing and flourishing are highly contested and contentious matters in society. What, she asks, might Christianity contribute at this critical point in the development of our understanding and practice, both social and personal? Her answer is elegantly written and will delight, surprise and perhaps sometimes shock. This is a deeply human grappling with the messy, chaotic realities and brokenness of life, which refuses the easy and idealized fictions of health as a pure and perfect state. Wellbeing is defined instead in terms of an ability to integrate harm, pain and suffering into a life that is open, transformed and transforming. It is, as she says in her concluding words, 'the stuff of love, mystery and miracles'.

ACKNOWLEDGEMENTS

As any writer knows, it's hard to complete a substantial project without *time*. I am indebted to my employers, the Diocese of Worcester, for the luxury of five weeks to dedicate wholeheartedly to this book. In particular, I would like to thank Bishops Peter Selby and David Walker, and the Diocesan Secretary, Robert Higham, for making this most important writing interlude possible. Thanks also to the wider Bishop's Staff team. At least two pieces of writing which have made their way, rewritten, into this book, were tried out first on them. Thanks to Peter Sedgwick for making the time to read and comment on the work as it developed. Special appreciation is reserved for Richard Hyde, my assistant at the Board for Social Responsibility, for maintaining – with good humour and his usual exemplary efficiency – the work of the office in my absence.

Whilst I have written this book on wellbeing from the position of one who has lived (so far) a relatively healthy and pain-free life, I would like to extend my thanks to my friends who have offered to me their insights gained from rather different experiences. In particular, Jo Ind and Donald Eadie.

Other friends and colleagues offered their valued opinions at an early stage, commenting on the book proposal. Thanks to Leslie Griffiths, Bishop Michael Lewis and Rev Barry Jones for their particularly acute comments. Only they will be able to discern whether I took any notice, but I'm pretty sure I did! Ideas were generated from a conference in Worcester on health at which Lynne Friedli and Ian Wylie were speakers.

Thanks to them for their papers, from which I learned much. Thanks too to the hospital chaplains in the Diocese of Worcester for welcoming me to sit in on their meetings with the Bishop. These have been most educative. A big thank you must also go to colleagues in health and social services in Worcestershire and Dudley, especially to Alec Kendall, a visionary, compassionate, and imaginative advocate of holistic public health in Worcestershire.

Finally, thanks to the friends who have supported me through the writing process, especially Ben Okafor, Jenny Jones, Janice Price and David Morphy; and love and profound appreciation to my partner Alex for lifting me to a place where new creativity and self-belief were possible.

INTRODUCTION

I notice him because of the way he moves. He is quick, free, fluid, assured. As with other men of slight build, his shoulders are the fixed point from which all else flows – in this case, a rather unusual choice of garments – picked up in a charity shop, or an expensive designer outlet, it could be either – he has that kind of style. His body is loose and angular – all joints and limbs, but strangely invisible under his clothing. He is more evocation than material reality, more spectral than embodied, because at no point does his body interrupt the 'line' of the fabric of his clothing. He *is* the line. White shirt. Yellow-brown trousers. Large black coat. Every item several sizes too large. These descriptions say little, which is strangely appropriate because his clothes are at one and the same time worthy of note, but irrelevant. What matters is the way he *inhabits* them – the way he seems somehow *just himself* in them. I see also his sculpted face, high cheekbones and make-up: a 'New Romantic' shade of violet blusher; dramatic Kohl round the eyes. Make-up is all the more striking when worn in defiance by a man.

Words spring to mind – three of them: spare, energetic, creative. Three things I have always wanted to be:

Spare – light, unencumbered, economical, detachable, mercurial, able to move on (able to change).
Energetic – lithe, spirited, productive, fast, focused, intense, dissatisfied.
Creative – quirky, unconventional, imaginative, original.

Three things I had always wanted to be, that is, until I encountered alternatives: voluptuous, languorous, laid-back. In the face of these, I doubted the certainty of my previous ambitions:

Voluptuous – soft, curvy, enfolding, safe, sensuous, warm.
Languorous – relaxed, unfocused, lazy, fulfilled, satisfied.
Laid-back – unbusy, carefree, not wishing to be in control.

This is how it is twice a day – every day – the daily commute. Catching sight of an attractive person, an unusual thing, or overhearing a compelling conversation, excites a free-flow of thoughts and ideas, directionless, in stark contrast to the purposefulness around me. I walk against the majority – in the opposite direction to the crowd, like a pebble holding out against the force of a stream, selfhood eroded then reconstituted by the infinite possibilities of otherness. Here is a monotonous and exhausting – but also exhilarating – circularity. Here I encounter, over and over again, an infinite number of lives I will never live, faces I'll never have, relationships I will never be part of, communities and histories to which I will never belong, stories I will never inhabit, jobs and successes I will never achieve, despairs and anxieties I will never taste, misfortunes that will never befall me.

And the twice-daily question, which is never quite articulated, is this: how to hold on to self in the face of such difference? How to find and remain myself, how to focus on and be satisfied with – even liberated by – the inevitable and inescapable singularity of it? My life, my face, my relationships, my community, my history, my story, my jobs, my successes and achievements, my despair and anxiety, my misfortunes. How to be a person, a real flesh-and-blood person, not a million possibilities? How to be content and not restless – or how to decide whether or not restlessness is, after all, appropriate? How to be somewhere and not everywhere, against all the odds, against the tide?

This reflection may seem an odd place to begin a book on health and wellbeing. But I start here because I start with a universal: that everybody is someone. And only one. Each of us is constituted by what we are, but also by what we are not. We are shaped by how we feel about who we are and who we are not. We are defined by our possibilities and potentialities, and also by our limitations.

Every body is some body. And no body is perfect. We inhabit, as human beings, a bewildering diversity and array of physical possibility in terms of mobility, fitness, flexibility, acuteness of consciousness and immediacy of senses. Being conscious is being conscious of physicality – from the moment we wake till the moment we return to sleep (and even, come to think of it, in sleep) we 'feel ourselves' and that 'feeling' is physical, mental and emotional all at the same time. All of us are vulnerable to stress, depression and anxiety, and all of us have some capacity for joy, pleasure and delight. We live lives that are a mixture of all of these things: lives in the balance, with the balance constantly changing. Most of us want to feel better, to look better, to be better, to be well. And we each mean something different by that. In contemporary health and social care jargon everyone has physical, mental and spiritual health needs.

Being well, or not being well, is perhaps the single most important aspect of human be-ing. It affects how we make and maintain relationships with those around us: strangers, lovers, colleagues, friends, family; how and whether we do our work and what kind of work we do. It determines the possibilities we have of getting out of ourselves through other forms of activity: play, leisure, exercise, art, fun. This book explores the nature of 'health' and of 'wellbeing' – the overlap between these two concepts, and the space between them. They are not synonymous. It explores individual experiences of these concepts but also – just as importantly – social, cultural, political and religious significances. This book is born of a mixture of theory, reflection, experience and practical engagements. It arises, as most such projects do, from a mixture of the personal and the professional.

In the mid-1990s I wrote a book about women's experiences of sexuality and embodiment within different contexts of

institutional Christianity.[1] The research involved long discussions and talks with a number of women: happy, celebratory,
sad, defeated, liberated, despairing, hopeful, passionate and
burnt-out. Though it was not a focus of the book, I noticed that
the women concerned had, in terms of their wellbeing, fared
very differently in the face of their experiences. Some were
resilient and others were not. Some held life together and
others did not. Some fell apart temporarily and others in a
more long-term way. I witnessed the links between physical
wellness and psychological wellness. I saw self-belief and self-
confidence written on some bodies, and self-denigration and
self-doubt written on others. I glimpsed, I think, something of
the depth and lifelong impact of the trauma of abuse – sexual
and spiritual – experienced by some. As I learned about the
dynamics of institutional power, and became more and more
familiar with the subtleties and textures of injustice, so I
became increasingly angry. This anger was, I realize now, in
large part determined by my perception that oppressive institutional Christianity was making women sick, and nobody
seemed to care. By extension, of course (and as many were
quick to remind me), it was obvious that it was also making
many men sick too, but at the time this was not my focus. In
short, it seemed to me, the churches were purveyors of ill-
health. And to make things worse, they were such while
simultaneously promoting themselves as agents of liberation
and healing for all. The reality of bodies and the reality of relationships seemed to be beyond the remit of churches in many
of the stories I heard.

  This latent and implicit health dimension to my work back
then was a thread I wasn't aware of at the time. Now I want
to trace these threads further back still. I remember the
emotional impact of hearing the stories of distress. The mixed
feelings they evoked in me; the desire simultaneously to
empathize and to disassociate. One survivor of sexual abuse
told me how she went to morning prayer at her local church
every day, and cried through the whole service. Day after
day. And morning after morning nobody, clergy or lay, came
to ask her why. She had once talked about her feelings of self-

annihilation to the vicar, but his response was that it was time to 'stop being angry and to move on'. Apparently then, there were clergy operating with a model of pastoral care which had a clear 'sell-by date' and this enraged me. At the same time, though, I was thinking to myself, 'But it can't be good to be like this forever, can it?' Well – can it?

Looking back, I now realize that hovering somewhere on the periphery of my consciousness at that time was the phrase, 'Aren't you better yet?' Hard to admit that such a thought was there, however distant. But now I have, I can recall it everywhere, in many contexts – over and over. It is the social voice that has shaped my personal reality. This social voice says that health and happiness are 'normal' – we have a right to them. Illness and distress are aberrations and must be eradicated – as quickly as possible. Everybody is ill from time to time, but not for long, and the sooner everything gets back to normal, the better. When they don't, it seems that all we can think of to say, corporately, is, 'Aren't you better yet?' And so now I recall, and want to explore in this book, the feelings of discomfort, impatience and embarrassment which have accompanied many of my encounters with illness and distress: my own and that of others. The sell-by date of sympathy is not the same for everybody, but most people operate with one. Ill for a day? Poor you. Ill for a week? Don't worry, we'll cover for you. Ill for a month? Aren't you better yet? Upset about a relationship break-up? Poor you, take all the time you need – this is big stuff. Still upset six months later? Isn't it time you moved on? Aren't you better yet?

As someone who has enjoyed, so far and for the most part, a high level of physical and psychological wellbeing I am, nevertheless, acutely aware of how fragile 'health' is, and how fragile 'wellbeing' is too. I do not underestimate the importance of my own temporary wellness to my self-definition and self-understanding, though I'm certain I do not fully appreciate this. Nevertheless, I am aware of my own emotional responses to episodes of physical weakness and imperfection when they have struck me, and I am aware (and often ashamed) of the limits in my abilities to deal with illness in others. This unwillingness and inability to cope with inactivity is not, I am sure, simply a case of an overdose of the Protestant work ethic in my upbringing (though admittedly that plays a part). Ridiculous adverts on the TV for remedies that apparently enable 'real men' to be macho businessmen-as-usual while in the grip of the flu are indicative of a wider social aspiration towards physical omnipotence.

These social attitudes are what I want to get to the bottom of (or at least begin to explore) in Chapters 1 and 2 of this book. Focusing on illness, wellness, disease, death and health, I will explore how these function in our social, political, cultural and symbolic world. If we *are* the stories that we tell ourselves, as individuals and communities, then there must be better stories – better values to hold on to – than those of late western capitalism which says that individual productivity is all that each and every one of us is worth; that illness must be 'combated' because it undermines people's ability to work and therefore to have an identity. And it is worth asking, too, how our religious stories are functioning: to underscore predominant utilitarian social attitudes by giving them spiritual backing, or to challenge them by offering alternative systems of belonging.

Nearly four years ago I took up my post as the Social Responsibility Officer for the Anglican Diocese of Worcester. Social Responsibility posts are diverse, unfocused affairs, but – most briefly and simply put – their aim is to facilitate, encourage and provide a focus for engagement by the Church in the big wide world. Having worked on the 'narrow' issue of sexuality, I anticipated a much broader professional remit, and was not disappointed. But, funnily enough, it was not long before health and wellbeing threads again began to emerge. Let me give just a couple of examples.

Part of the job of Social Responsibility Officer entails offering advice and support where necessary to local community-based initiatives and projects. The first such project that I visited was called the 'Lighthouse', located on an estate, characterized by high levels of economic deprivation, in Halesowen. It was a simple enough idea: a community flat offering unconditional acceptance and a safe space for residents to drop in and seek support and social contact. No pressure. No hidden agendas. On that day, and every time I have visited since, I encountered a warmth of welcome that I have rarely felt anywhere. There was a feeling of safety and sanctuary.

Four years on, the project has expanded hugely, with four other 'Lighthouses' in other parts of the West Midlands. The formula remains the same: to provide a safe, unconditionally welcoming space to women, men and children in the locality. There is childcare, food, drink, friendship, and a range of classes to attend for those who choose to: 'stressbusters', for instance, and skills for living. This project has had a major impact on the locality: on the health of individuals, and on social cohesion. It works because the project somehow enables people to believe in themselves; to build, slowly, through small and gradual steps, the self-esteem that has been systematically crushed by their life experience. So it has become clear to me, through projects like this, that the single most significant interventions in urban regeneration are not matters of bricks and mortar (though material facilities are immensely important), but those which enable self-belief and the building of self-esteem. Wellbeing – individual or communal – is impossible without it. And building it is a purely human, relational, task.

The other early example was my first visit to a prison – a women's prison, HMP Brockhill. My task was to lead a Sunday evening service in the chapel. I was extremely nervous at the prospect, and had no idea what to expect. What I found was a bunch of young women – mostly older adolescents, many with children of their own, interested to meet a stranger and eager to tell me about their children and hear about mine (I was a disappointment, not having any!). One of their fellow inmates had committed suicide that week, and many were incredibly distressed about this and desperate to light candles in her memory. This was a difficult experience – an odd mix of familiarity and strangeness: the familiarity of being inside an institution surrounded by other women; the strangeness that this was a prison, and that most of the women were from a completely different social background from mine. But never before had I been faced so starkly, and in such a concentrated way, with material evidence of how class and economic differences get written on the body. White, middle-class women are not, by and large, to be found in prisons. Only poor women go to prison. Prisons are unhealthy places, and prisoners are unhealthy people. Mostly unhealthy before they are incarcerated, but certainly not helped – either physically or psychologically – by the experience. I knew that in theory – but I didn't really expect it to be so in your face. There were so many obvious signs of eating disorders and self-harming, so many traces of old injuries, presumably at the hands of others – and, above all, signs of neglect, bad diet and lack of exercise. This was a different world, but also a recog-nizable one.

The other major area of my work, on which much of the reflection in this book will be built, is more policy-oriented. In the current political climate, the focus of a job such as mine is 'partnership working'. Larger, secular organizations now have 'partnership officers' – those whose job it is, in the era of joined-up government, to prioritize work with other agencies for common ends, with all the necessary networking and relationship-building that such working methods entail. Whether churches ever can or will restructure their staffing complement to fit the needs of the 'big wide world' rather than internal organizational habits is doubtful. But the tradi-tionally vague and all-encompassing umbrella of 'Social Responsibility' has lent itself, luckily, in many parts of the country, to prioritizing church contributions to inter-agency partnerships. My job description has long required that I 'engage with secular agencies in the area of social concern'. On taking up the post in 1998, participation in the nascent 'Worcestershire Partnership' offered, I considered, an excel-lent short cut to familiarity with the major players in one of the two Local Authority areas covered by the diocese. As the New Labour Government shaped its agenda for change, it became obvious that such partnerships were/are 'the only show in town' for achieving change – or, at least, for gaining funding for achieving change. Bringing together the private, public and third sectors, they promised a strategic and systematic approach to the regeneration and enrichment of our communities. As regionalization has taken hold, these sub-regional partnerships have become increasingly important, and many will become what are now known as LSPs (Local Strategic Partnerships), responsible for Community Plans – with, for the first time, a government requirement that faith communities be included in such plans for the future wellbeing and health of our communities.

Against this local political backdrop, a focus on health in my work evolved partly by serendipity, partly by design. I came into a context where close links and a well-established and creative partnership were already in place with various staff at the Health Authority – particularly in public health and health promotion. Added to this, the wider national policy context was opening up new possibilities for co-operation between faith communities and health professionals. As Helen Orchard points out in her recent collection, *Spirituality in Health Care Contexts*,

> In the last ten years in particular there has been something of a step change in the level of engagement with the spiritual care agenda by the health service. This has been the consequence of a range of factors; among them policy imperatives such as the Patient's Charter, the emergence of holistic philosophy of health care, and the growing interest of postmodern society in what is now commonly nicknamed 'Body Mind Spirit' matters. The welcome result for the NHS has been increased debate, improved training and education and a heightened level of awareness among a whole range of health care professionals about the importance of this dimension of care.[2]

The territory of 'spiritual care' will be explored in more detail later in the book. Interestingly, however, the pull towards faith community involvement in health issues came from other political quarters too. The Worcestershire Partnership decided, along with most other such partnerships, to focus on the following thematic areas in its work: community safety, social inclusion, economic development, lifelong learning, environmental sustainability, and health and wellbeing. In the face of perceived domination of the health and wellbeing agenda by the Health Authority (albeit for entirely under-standable and very practical reasons), those from other agencies expressed a desire for this area of work to be more broadly and holistically interpreted. Grappling for a term to express what exactly such a holistic concept of health encom-passed, one Local Authority member of the Partnership repeatedly settled on the phrase 'spiritual health' to sum up what was missing. This term was never any further defined, but functioned as a 'good enough' expression of intent to go beyond what the Health Authority and NHS encompass in their work. So the concept of spiritual health hung around in the air as a slightly exotic concept that no one could quite explain, but that united everybody behind a hunch there was something in it.

At the same time, the Health Authority was putting together its Health Improvement Programme, which seemed about as all-encompassing a project as one could imagine. With its focus on six district council areas and twelve thematic foci (for instance prison health, rural health, accident prevention, minority ethnic community health), this was a massive plan-ning and consultation exercise, and one in which church groups played a part. My conversations with Health Authority staff revealed many areas of common ground and interests, not least a strong emphasis on promoting equality in health. Clearly the question was how to focus resources on those who needed them most, who were currently being excluded, for a variety of reasons, from access to services. There was a recog-nition that to improve the average levels of health for every-body is not good enough – the real challenge is how to improve the health of the least well-off: those living in urban hot spots of deprivation, and those living in isolated poverty in rural areas. This led to joint work on the role of faith communities in the promotion of equality in health – with, most recently, a focus on mental health promotion. Such issues receive attention in Chapter 3, where I explore the potentialities and dynamics of church engagement at various levels with the health and wellbeing agenda.

During one of our conversations about the nature of partnership working, my Health Authority colleague asked me (in all innocence), 'Is the diocese a strategic organization?' Aside from any answer I might have given, the question itself felt like a joke. 'Strategic' and 'church' have never been natural bedfellows in my understanding of either. And I wondered, was this a good thing or a bad thing? But the nature of the question from 'an outsider', and my own emotional reactions to it, led me to reflect on this question and helped me to begin to identify some of the unease and ambivalence I have felt in representing the church in inter-agency working over the past few years. The latter parts of this book are born out of that perplexity.

Engagement has proved fruitful in many ways. But participation has also precipitated many questions about who 'we' (the Church) think we are in such contexts: what do we think we are doing; what do we think is being expected of us; what are we trying to achieve and how will we know if we've been successful? What do we think we can offer in partnership encounters? The received wisdom, oft-repeated (not least by Government ministers) is that faith communities and churches are key stakeholders because they can be the conduits between agencies seeking to instigate change and those at the grassroots who are crucial to making that change happen. Or, to put it another way, the Church is said to be the only organization with branches in every community, without exception, across the UK. In theory this is true. And in theory churches therefore do have much to offer. Again, however, such secular expectations impose upon us certain obligations, not least to be self-reflexive about how accurate this received wisdom really is. How inclusive, for instance, are these branches? How representative are they of the wider communities in which they are set?

In terms of ecclesiology, inter-agency working and participation in partnerships is about as theologically exciting and
challenging as it gets. Will it be the arena through which the
churches discover the uniqueness of our identity, or the one
in which we run for cover in shame because we are not like
everyone else? What are the areas where the big wide world
rightly challenges us to get our act together, and what are
we proud of? How can we be clear about and true to our
multiple mission as a faith community, while at the same
time recognizing that different identities are appropriate for
different functions? We need a lot more clarity, a lot more
courage and a lot more corporate sharing of expertise and
experience if we are to grasp the ecclesiological opportunities
that inter-agency working affords. Health and wellbeing
provide, in this book, a case study for working at some of
these important questions.

Above all, what happens to our theology in these
encounters – our theological rationale for involvement in the
first place, and the theology which emerges from our activities? What happens to our understanding of God?

In an article in the journal *Political Theology*, Stephen Pattison
characterizes contemporary theology as 'a kind of whispered
conversation on matters esoteric conducted in a foreign
language behind closed doors in a distant attic'.[3] Pattison is
here highlighting the, I think incontrovertible, fact that there is
a growing division between theological and secular language
and concepts. Christocentric, ecclesiastical language is no
longer effective when we try to contribute to the wider
marketplace of ideas. He goes on to call for a new vision for
public theology which 'should address issues of general
public concern, in a genuinely public arena, in a publicly
accessible way, using publicly comprehensible concepts and
mechanisms. This with a view to effecting some kind of transformation of public views, policies and actions.'[4] This, of
course, is easy to say but fiendishly difficult to achieve. A key
focus for Chapter 3 of this book is an exploration of the notion
of 'translation' – as a means of introducing insights from a
specific faith-community base into the general common

language of public discourse – with accompanying reflections on what changes such translations might demand in our understanding of Christian identity.

What resources can we discern in the faith tradition: the unconditional value of each human being, the gift of life itself? What is the meaning of this in a world of unflourishing? This is not at all straightforward. It's easy to say that Christianity is 'for health'; that Christianity has always believed in health and human wellbeing. But that wouldn't be the whole story. As explored already in this introduction, churches can promote sickness too. But the Church doesn't always, and doesn't have to, make people sick. One reason for writing this book is a firm and passionate belief on my part that the opposite is the case. Nevertheless, while Christianity has expressed a belief in health through, for example, the building of hospitals, it has shown the opposite in the mortification of the flesh, in undermining the material body as being of less importance than the purity of the disembodied soul. This ambivalence has been at the centre of Christian traditions: the glorification of human beings as the peak achievement of God's creativity, and the denigration of them as mere miserable offenders; the value of each one of us as minute but immensely important to God, and the dwarfing of us as insignificant in the divine scheme of things. Which interpretation of the way things are is 'true' is not so important as the fact that both have existed, side by side. And that both have existed for a reason. As we dive into the complexity of the contemporary health and wellbeing scene, there is a need to remember a range of Christian histories, rather than to use biblical or historical precedent to support us in a single interpretation. We might just miss something vital. There is not one simple message but many Christian messages.

In the same article Pattison makes a dozen suggestions for 'transcending irrelevance and marginalization'. A key one is that theologians and church people need to work to make theology a more truly imaginative and innovative activity that is universally accessible. 'For example', he says, 'it may be possible to create new religious stories that are not the old stories in new words but are actually new stories that have some indebtedness to the old.'[5]

This brings me to my own theological methodology. My own position is as something of an exile from traditional theology – its language and methods. At some point I seem to have fallen out of its particular loop of meaning. Somehow the self-referential linguistic circularity of most contemporary theology leaves me unmoved and unaffected. It explains very little to me and offers few tools for analysis of the world I experience every day. So I tend to look to cultural theorists and others for those intellectual tools. Yet their work is, in turn, most useful when it resonates with the religious language that is my heritage and the questions of ultimate meaning and value which I still pursue. I find it instructive and empowering that a theologian central to establishment theological endeavour in this country, Daniel Hardy, should say that 'we need to learn to think of Christian faith as by nature *spread out*, as something *extended* by its "spread-out-ness". At first, that seems to run against the grain, because we are so much accustomed to think in terms of the concentrations of Christian faith in Bible, church, beliefs and certainties.'[6]

There is little in this book which could pass for 'concentrations of Christian faith in Bible, church, beliefs and certainties'. There is much exploration of theological 'spread-out-ness'. Some readers will no doubt think it so spread out as not to qualify as 'theology' at all. Such judgements rest in the mind's-eye of the beholder, of course. For my part, this book represents an attempt to participate, in places (usually through reflections at the beginning of each section), in narrative theology. By which I mean, to pick up Pattison again, there are attempts in this book to 'tell new stories that have some indebtedness to the old'. These stories and reflections are inspired by experience (though they are not attempts to describe faithfully that experience). They represent my attempts to take key pieces of scriptural text or key religious practices, to semi-detach them from their traditional contexts, invest them with new meaning, and perhaps shed some new light upon them. I don't know what to call the result, and in a sense it doesn't matter. They are simply a device to encourage the reader to relate to issues in a way that engages the emotions as well as the intellect.

1

WELL?

I have called you by name, you are mine.
(Isaiah 43: 1)

'Obese, unkempt Caucasian.' That's what they called Sarah at the inquest, according to her mother. 'But to me, she was still my daughter,' she said. And to me, she was still my friend. She was my friend and I couldn't help her.

Her death was, in some ways, quick. She killed herself in just fifteen minutes. A deliberately chosen, well-planned use of the maximum amount of time allotted to her to be alone. In other ways, though, it was the longest and slowest death – death by severe, debilitating, seemingly inescapable mental illness.

She wasn't always 'obese' – the drugs did that. And when she was well, she was never 'unkempt' – quite the opposite. This is what she was like: bold, courageous, sensitive, intelligent, generous, humorous, charming, persuasive, incisive, persistent, volatile, rebellious and stubborn.

The impact of institutions was stamped on her being: the military had shaped her family life; a boarding school her childhood and adolescence; the mental health system her short adulthood. All in their own ways brutal, fostering dependence in exchange for security, then failing to fulfil their side of the bargain. She became dependent, but they were not dependable. Or at least if they were, it was not enough.

One day she said to me, 'I am unfit for human habitation.' But her only option was to inhabit herself anyway – courageously, for as long as she could manage it. Yet in many ways she was a 'light' person – wearing the impact of institutionalization not as victim but as resister. Apparently on her thirty-second birthday, just ten days before her death, she was ordering take-away pizza for herself and her friends on the ward. Sitting in laceless shoes, surrounded by those with whom she'd made a connection, scoffing. Just like 'before' (or was there a 'before'?).

Sarah's death flings me back like no other. Back to school, when we were close; when she was happier. I remember the late nights, the long walks, the meaning-of-life talks. She could be scary even then, sometimes – the times when her pursuit of meaning took her so deep into herself that I worried she'd never re-emerge, never re-connect, never come back. Perhaps all the warning signs were there, even then. Perhaps we should have seen it coming long before we did.

This death flings me back also to that endless puzzle: what was wrong with Sarah? How come none of us could help her – fix things for her? Occasionally she would get in touch by phone when she was feeling well enough. Plans would be made to meet up, but these were nearly always superseded by relapses. It was as though we were calling to one another across a no-man's land of time and experience, across a massive gap of incomprehension – inhabiting different worlds but aware of the need, somehow, to keep in touch. But the divergence was too great, and it was always accelerating.

Introducing 'wellbeing'

Writing this reflection I began to realize that Sarah was, in large part, responsible for my attempts to get to grips with concepts of 'health' and 'wellbeing'. Mental health is a mystery. It cannot be caused – only fostered. Mental illness is scary to those of us who have not experienced it ourselves. Living in its hinterland demands tolerance of the inexplicable and not too much reliance on the explicable. There are persistent questions which seem to have no answer: is it true that sometimes there is simply nothing we can do? Are there times in relationships when we are powerless? Or is that just an excuse? These are the questions that exercised me when Sarah was alive, and which she has left me with now that she is dead. This section explores the meanings of health and wellbeing – particularly in the context in which we find ourselves in early twenty-first-century northern European western capitalism. But I want to embrace these larger themes by way of further reflection on Sarah.

They say that when babies and young children die, it's the size of the coffin at the funeral that leaves the attenders undone. The smallness represents an unbearable poignancy. At Sarah's funeral the size of the coffin was unbearably poignant for the opposite reason. It was huge. She was tall, yes, but it was the width of the coffin that I hadn't anticipated. It had been months since I'd last seen her – and I had been surprised at how much weight she had gained then – but she had obviously gained a lot more since. There was something shocking about the way in which this symbolized, at the point of death, the complex interweaving of the physical and the psychological. Who we are, psychologically, is written on our bodies physically, and who we become, physically, affects our psychological wellbeing.

Let me explore this further. Sarah was, in large part, a solitary person. She had a few very close friends. Much was demanded of us, and much was offered in return. But overwhelmingly, she was alone in the world: by choice or necessity, who knows? This was a psychological fact that had very definite material outworkings. It meant, for instance, that she didn't much like team sports – though she did like exercise, so mostly her preference was just to walk, for miles. Usually alone, but sometimes with a close friend or, in the holidays, with her dog. So her physique was one of a walker, in contrast to that of, say, a hockey player or a squash player. In other words, her personality showed. A second example: Sarah had very definite likes and dislikes, and this applied especially to food. She did not eat ordinary combinations of food, and she did not eat in conventional places. Instead, she preferred to hoard the things that she liked, to eat alone in the way she preferred. Her choices were not always healthy ones: too much bread and cheese and too many chocolate digestives – not enough hot meals with vegetables! In short, she ate very specifically – and with very definite enthusiasms. Her food choices were also written on her body. She was usually neither too fat nor too thin, but her weight was subject to oscillation, even then.

In order to speak of Sarah at the funeral, I had been consciously calling up memories of our school days, with the help of other friends. I had sat with all the photos I had of her spread out in front of me, re-familiarizing myself with how she was. Her hospital chaplain thought it would be good for family and friends to hear someone speak of a time when she was not defined – as she was in the end – almost exclusively by what was wrong with her. 'We all need to be reminded', he said, 'that there was more to Sarah than her illness.' I was sure he was right, and it wasn't hard to recall how she was. But as I brought forth the images from the past, I was struck as much by the continuity between the past and the present, as by the discontinuity and difference. How she was when she died seemed an exaggerated version of certain aspects of how she was when she was a schoolgirl, aspects which had all but eclipsed other elements of who she was then. It became clear to me that in the intervening period between the photographs being taken and the time of her death, she had been *living out an active dialogue with her history*. I don't claim to know a great deal about who Sarah was before I became close to her, or of the childhood and adolescent experiences which predated the ones she shared with me. But she told me something of them, and I remember some of what she told me. The key insight is that, as with each and every one of us, Sarah lived with and in and through her personal history, with its complex mix of positive possibility and negative potential for harm.

Another insight from Sarah's experience strikes me as important at the beginning of an exploration of human well-being. That is, the importance of relationships, which can either constitute the very foundations of living well or represent a major corrosive force undermining any likelihood of achieving a sense of wellbeing. Sarah did not put her trust in others easily, but when she did it was firm and whole-hearted. One of her teachers in particular elicited this trust from her, and she worked at his subject with a level of engagement and dedication that went beyond school-report 'diligence'. You can be 'diligent' for anyone. You can be dedicated only for love and trust and admiration. Sarah was a devoted, attentive and tactile friend, and friendships seemed to be the key to her flourishing. Whenever she got into sexual relationships, on the other hand, she became edgy, volatile, changeable and defensive. She began to take unnecessary risks – becoming reckless while asserting her right, in the face of any challenge by her friends, to be herself and to do what she wanted. It was as though some relationships held her stable and rooted, and other relationships (especially those with lovers) threw her into instability and danger. Part of her was attracted to this danger – another part couldn't cope with it.

Finally, reflecting on Sarah's story furnishes me with insights about identity and its part in human wellbeing. 'Obese, unkempt Caucasian' was somebody's summary of her identity at the time that she died. Presumably this is what passes for fact in the medical profession. But this description was not recognized by those who loved and cared for Sarah as either neutral or factual. It was quite simply a merciless and foreign designation that rendered her dehumanized and unrecognizable. This designation came after her death, of course, but I wonder what other designations she lived with during her ten years or more of illness? The last time I saw her it was clear that her life had become, to her, a list of things she thought she would never do: hold down a job, live independently, cook meals for herself, ride her bike, have another relationship, have children.

But this list said nothing of her achievements: her intelligence, her musicality, her travel abroad, her successful friendships based on an extraordinary level of empathy coupled with an assertive determination to speak her mind. It said nothing of the achievement simply of survival in the face of endless setbacks as she tried so hard to be well again. Likewise, her list made no mention of her extraordinary spirituality or her hard-won faith journey. She had always been a 'spiritual' person – by which I mean she had always been bothered by questions of ultimate meaning and value, though her upbringing had not been religious. At school, the time of my friendship with her encompassed my keenest churchgoing years and sometimes she used to come along too. She found this faith at one and the same time both attractive and alien. Once she spoke of her yearning to experience what she observed others experiencing in church – of wanting to 'belong'; to share the common belief system, to feel part of something bigger, something beyond herself. Later, she did embrace Christianity and the Church, and I believe this was helpful to her.

Having reflected on Sarah's story, let me restate the resulting preliminary observations about what constitutes human wellbeing. It seems that it has to do with the interweaving of the psychological, the physical and the spiritual; it includes an element of how we inhabit our personal histories and how we negotiate these in our present; it depends upon our inter-relationship with others – relationships which offer the possibility of harm and of flourishing – and, finally, it involves questions of identity. Wellbeing must be about naming oneself, not being named by others; naming our limitations as we understand them, not as others do. And living with them, while also extending ourselves in ways that do not undermine our naming.

The context of our wellbeing

Further exploration of what we mean by 'wellbeing' and 'health' demands a closer look at the context within which our twenty-first-century bodies, hearts, minds and spirits live and move and have their being.

Look around you now. What do you see (if you can see)? How do you see it? What do you hear (if you can hear)? How do you hear it? If you move easily, what is to hand? Let me tell you what I see and hear and feel. I sit at a laptop which is now warm under my hands, and buzzes busily (this worries me a little, as I'm not sure it should do that). I have no idea what signals it is emitting and whether these are friendly or damaging. I see the screen clearly because I wear contact lenses – or, occasionally, glasses. I hear the noise my laptop makes because I am enabled to do so with the help of a hearing aid. I write – form words, by utilizing the keyboard of my laptop, a prosthetic device which becomes a natural extension of my internal world: my thoughts and feelings and sense-making rationality. My mobile phone is on the other side of the room (and I'm glad it's some way away because I'm sure it's also emitting signals and waves which may be harmful in ways I do not understand). Occasionally it beeps when a friend sends me a text message. I enjoy these. Sometimes it rings – but I experience such calls as rather unwelcome intrusions. I'm very unlikely to answer it unless it's someone *really* special. Every now and again, when I get bored with communicating with you, the imagined reader, I cross the room to plug my laptop into a phone line to connect to my emails. These come steadily, though haphazardly, and demand instant attention, however busy I am with other things.

When I got up this morning I had a bath and, as usual, used at least half a dozen different cosmetic products, all complex chemical compounds and the result of years of research and development (shampoo, conditioner, shower gel, deodorant, moisturizer, hair mousse, hair gel). Not to mention the make-up. I am dressed in several items of clothing, some of supposedly 'natural' fabric (cotton), and others made of fleece – high-tech and lightweight which I believe can be made of recycled washing-up-liquid bottles (though I don't think my garments are that politically correct). These items of clothing are 'prosthetics' too: they become part of me when I put them on. They move with me – and in an important sense they *are* me, as long as I wear them. I have three body-piercings, all in the earlobes (you may be relieved to know: I certainly am), so my body is not 'as nature intended it'. Soon, if NHS waiting lists ever get short enough, I will have one of the tiny bones in my ear replaced by a little piece of metal. Then my body will, arguably, be even less as nature intended it. Though with luck I will then no longer need the hearing aid.

Later, when I have written enough words today to deserve it, I will leave the flat and travel – probably by another prosthetic device, my car – to see a friend, to communicate in yet another medium (face-to-face talking, a curiously old-fashioned device but no less inviting or pleasurable for that). This will help me to connect with something beyond the currently mixed-up contents of my own head. We will probably eat food and drink wine which originate from another part of the world – which have clocked up thousands of what are now termed 'food miles' to end up on a table in Islington, and this will all be served to us by several people of a number of ethnic origins and socio-cultural experiences. Once I've left the restaurant, I will probably remember absolutely nothing about them.

'By the late twentieth century, our time, a mythic time, we are all chimeras, theorized and fabricated hybrids of machine and organism; in short, we are cyborgs. The cyborg is our ontology; it gives us our politics.'[1] So says feminist scientist and epistemologist Donna Haraway in a book published way back in 1991. If we, as humans, could be said then to have a cyborg ontology, this must be all the more true now, over ten years later. She goes on to assert that 'Late twentieth-century machines have made thoroughly ambiguous the difference between natural and artificial, mind and body, self-developing and externally designed, and many other distinctions that used to apply to organisms and machines. *Our machines are disturbingly lively, and we ourselves frighteningly inert*'.[2] (italics mine)

Let's look in more depth at the reality of cyborg existence. We live, as cyborgs, with the delusion of transparent communication, the illusion of constant availability and the hope of perfect safety and security. We imagine that help is always at hand. All we need do is phone or text a friend, or the emergency services, or the car breakdown company. The ubiquitous mobile phone is great, of course, unless the train crashes, or the plane is blown out of the sky – or we forget to recharge the battery. Only then is the fragility of our communication systems exposed, along with our personal vulnerability and the precariousness of what might have passed for security.

So how are our identities textured by the vagaries of these new forms of communication? On the plus side, we are offered a fuller range of contact possibilities. There is no longer necessarily a need to be with those with whom we share physical proximity, for we might rather 'be with' those who are far away. Communities are now virtual as well as geographical. The down side is that this can afford a heightened and more acute sense of loneliness. Once the computer is turned off and the mobile has gone quiet (because everyone has more important things to do and other people to see), we are on our own. This isolation can hit us all the more forcefully when it is experienced in contrast to a virtual babble of communication busyness. The silence feels strange. And even in the midst of the Babel of modern communication, all is not necessarily relationally well. The potential for misunderstanding is great as we rely on communication systems which progressively filter our thoughts and feelings through fewer and fewer media. The phone long ago deprived us of eye-contact. Texting and email now deprive us of the subtlety carried by vocal inflections. Put this together with the speed-to-aid-efficiency which is the raison d'être of these communication systems and we are in dangerous as well as exciting territory. This is a minimalist communication-universe. Love and obsession can (and do) grow voraciously in shallow soil where they are not intended to flourish; resentments and regrets spring from messages whose brevity can communicate a devastating indifference that was never intended. We have already discovered that relationships are key to human wellbeing. Who we are becoming to one another as cyborgs in a high-tech context is therefore an important question for us. Are we becoming simply virtual empty promises with no material or emotional substance? Or are we bringing into being a richer, more complex repertoire of relationships, many-layered and multi-textured, and are we feeling all the more fulfilled for that? And if so, who are the 'we' who have access to these possibilities? In my experience, each new method of communication brings with it new possibilities for caring and (dare I say it) praying for and with one another. Yet it also brings about new possibilities for exclusionary practices.

All of which brings me back to Donna Haraway, who reminds us that, 'The main trouble with cyborgs, of course, is that they are the illegitimate offspring of militarism and patriarchal capitalism, not to mention state socialism. But illegitimate offspring are often exceedingly unfaithful to their origins. Their fathers, after all, are inessential.'[3]

In other words, in terms of our corporate history, the origins of our contemporary cyborg existence are ethically extremely suspect. However, what we do with our patriarchal capitalist inheritance is up to us. It is clear that we cannot sum up and simplify our cyborg existence as either unproblematically 'good' or straightforwardly 'bad'. For the ethical landscape in which we now find ourselves is as subtly textured as our relational and emotional one. Global capitalism is the single most important factor affecting any attempt, individual or corporate, to negotiate an ethical way through this landscape. Whether we like it or not everyone, to some extent, lives lives that are shaped by its values and conditioned by its reflexes.

As long ago as the 1970s Michael Wilson wrote a groundbreaking book entitled *Health is for People,* in which he got to grips with the practical and pastoral theological challenge of health issues in the modern world. Interestingly, his words then perfectly sum up our situation now, nearly thirty years later, as we contemplate the meaning of human inter-relatedness in a postmodern context of global capitalism: 'We compete, in fact, for hygiene resources. Anyone who is able to say, "I have enough" or "I am well" must then go on to ask "At cost to whom have I enough?" "At cost to whom am I well?" '[4] We are, certainly, brought up short in our discussions about laptops and mobile phones by the reminder of statistics which seem to have been forever with us: the billions worldwide who lack primary health care, the growing millions in developing countries – particularly in sub-Saharan Africa – who are HIV-positive with very little, if any, available resources for drug treatments, and the millions who lack access to clean drinking water and enough food to live on. This is compounded by the economic power wielded by the 'first world' – particularly the USA – because of the policies which developing nations are forced to adopt in order to gain an albeit crude unequal access to the global marketplace.

These issues are compellingly explored by Cliff Marrs, who writes:

> 11 September was a kairos day for the rich, fatalities at the World Trade Centre currently stand at 3,045 with another 500 missing presumed dead, but for the world's poor it was just another day of death . . . On 11 September c.45,000 died, most from preventable causes and diseases: malnutrition, diarrhoea, measles, malaria, TB, Aids, polluted water and air, and poor sanitation. Guy Dauncy observes: "the pain of death in New York is no different from the pain of death [elsewhere] . . . our hearts all suffer in the same way".[5]

While the impact of global capitalism on human health and wellbeing across the world is a hugely important issue, it is beyond the remit of this book. However, what is important here is some consideration of the ways in which macro-economic forces are shaping popular understandings and expectations of health and wellbeing closer to home.

Novelist and social commentator Jeanette Winterson draws our attention to a most important issue when she says, 'I do not think it an exaggeration to say that most of the energy of most of the people is being diverted into a system which destroys them. Money is no antidote. If the imaginative life is to be renewed it needs its own coin.'[6] She continues her sharp critique of 'money culture' as follows:

Money culture recognises no currency but its own. Whatever is not money, whatever is not making money, is useless to it. The entire efforts of our government as directed through our society are efforts towards making more and more money. This favours the survival of the dullest. This favours those who prefer to live in a notional reality where goods are worth more than time and where things are more important than ideas.[7]

Winterson is not simply saying that material wellbeing isn't everything and that money can't buy you happiness (though she is saying that). She is, crucially, calling to our attention the need to recognize and prioritize the imaginative life and the arts because, in her words, 'the arts stimulate and satisfy a part of our nature that would otherwise be left untouched . . . the emotions art arouses in us are of a different order to those aroused by experience of any other kind.'[8] She speaks prophetically, inspiring us to see art not as an add-on luxury, important to human wellbeing only after all our material needs have been met, but as necessity; she inspires us to see art as very much like religion:

> Art is visionary; it sees beyond the view from the window, even though the window is its frame. This is why the arts fare much better alongside religion than alongside either capitalism or communism. The god-instinct and the art-instinct both apprehend more than the physical bio-logical material world. The artist need not believe in God, but the artist does consider reality as multiple and complex.[9]

The ultimate implication is that the wellbeing brought about by art is not an easy wellbeing, but a most challenging one: 'Art is not documentary . . . its true effort is to open to us dimensions of the spirit and of the self that normally lie smothered under the weight of living.'[10] And again, 'We know we are dissatisfied, but the satisfactions that we seek come at a price beyond the resources of a money culture. Can we afford to live imaginatively, contemplatively? Why have we submitted to a society that tries to make imagination a privilege when to each of us it comes as a birthright?'[11]

Winterson suggests an intriguing alliance between religion and art that we will return to in the conclusion of this book. In the meantime, the most important message is that in a context of global capitalism, it is easy to be caught up in the illusion that human wellbeing can be purchased by the currency of money alone. Winterson reminds us that, human identity being as complex as it is, there are aspects to wellbeing that demand a different currency – the currency of the imagination: a different coin.

Let's look more closely at another of Winterson's ideas – we are valuing that which is destroying us. In his huge but hugely readable recent book, *The Noonday Demon: An Anatomy of Depression*, Andrew Solomon offers the following observations on the corrosive potential of our postmodern cyborg context:

The climbing rates of depression are without question the consequence of modernity. The pace of life, the technological chaos of it, the alienation of people from one another, the breakdown of traditional family structures, the loneliness that is endemic, the failure of systems of belief (religious, moral, political, social – anything that seemed once to give meaning and direction to life) have been catastrophic. Fortunately, we have developed systems for coping with the problem. We have medications that address the organic disturbances, and therapies that address the emotional upheavals of chronic diseases. Depression is an increasing cost for our society, but it is not ruinous. We have the psychological equivalents of sunscreens and baseball hats and shade.

But do we have the equivalent of an environmental movement, a system to contain the damage we are doing to the social ozone layer? That there are treatments should not cause us to ignore the problem that is treated. We need to be terrified by the statistics. What is to be done? Sometimes it seems that the rate of illness and the number of cures are in a sort of competition to see which can outstrip the other.[12]

Solomon echoes powerfully some themes which have already been touched upon here. He too, for instance, points to the importance of human relationships, and the need for an identity – a meaning and purpose to life. While he may be right that the cost to our society represented by depression may not yet be ruinous, Sarah's story has demonstrated that the cost to individuals can certainly be so. And story upon story in Solomon's book, not least that of his own experience, more than bear this out. His next move, though, is to point us to a consideration of the underlying causes of the damage to our 'social ozone layer'. What is it about the dynamics of modern life that feeds the personal destruction that we see all around us: that Winterson hints at and that Solomon reinforces?

If the only valid currency our society values and recognizes is the money-making currency, then by extension the only people who will really be valued are those that can earn a living by being productive. This means, firstly, that anyone who is economically unproductive (to use a phrase from within the linguistic repertoire of money-making) is pretty much useless. Age and wisdom are useless. Reflection and contemplation are useless. Art and recreation are useless except insofar as they enable otherwise useful people a 'restorative window' in their lives to 'recharge their batteries' (note the phrase) so that they can more effectively return to the money-making fray.

Michael Wilson was again bang up-to-date thirty years ago when he explored the logical outcome of this way of thinking:

What then is our role? What then is our value? Few people with experience in the care of older people would disagree with the statement that one of the most important factors in the maintenance of health at all ages is a sense of personal worth, of being wanted. A sense of one's own identity. There is no group of people in greater confusion about their identity or civic worth than the elderly, for they approach with uncertain steps the mystery of death which is the ultimate threat to our self and to our meaning.[13]

Wilson also raises here the symbolic importance of perceived nearness to death, an issue to which we will return shortly. For now, it is enough to note his reinforcement of the notion that a sense of personal worth and identity are key to wellbeing. In our social context, therefore, we can begin to see why exclusion from the marketplace of economic activity and productivity have potentially devastating results.

But the implications go even wider than this. If wellbeing is tied up with feelings of self-worth, then it has to be noted that these feelings of self-worth are in turn brought about by perceptions of individual achievement and success. But in a competitive society, almost by definition, not everyone can be successful. Our predominant social value system has, therefore, a way of deciding who are the most likely people to be successful (i.e., money-making) people. Ultimately, you have to have the right kind of body and the right kind of look. 'Achieving' fitness and health are important to this, as will be explored in a moment. But note the circularity of the argument: to be healthy you need to feel worthy, to feel worthy you need to be successful, to be successful you need to be healthy.

The interweaving of social and spiritual pressures to attain a certain kind of embodiment are explored brilliantly, and with a rare clarity and honesty, in Jo Ind's *Fat is a Spiritual Issue*, which focuses on her experience of living with an eating disorder:

My hand pinched the fat that was forming around my less definite chin line. I watched myself squeeze my newly rounded cheeks and felt my fingernails press into the flesh that covered them. Looking at myself was not enough. The fact that I was disgusting had to be confirmed by touch as well.[14]

> I started to get undressed, pulled my dress off and then my shirt, looking with disgust at my protruding breasts and extended belly. I grimaced at the white, fleshy thighs, enhanced for extra ugliness with stretchmarks. I was loathsome to myself.[15]

The self-hatred she describes is, in her case, brought about by her perception that she is 'too fat'. But her description of the dynamics of self-loathing will be appreciated by many readers, for most of us, I would argue, have experienced something similar at some time in our lives, for a variety of reasons and to a variety of degrees. The structural inequalities of racism, sexism, class bias and homophobia make intense experiences of self-hatred more common among some social groupings than others, but the possibility is real for all of us. Women, in particular, are vulnerable to self-loathing because of our size and shape, a fact borne out by Jo Ind's experience:

> As I became more open about my eating disorder, other people told me about theirs. I was amazed at the number of beautiful women of all different shapes and sizes who said that they hated their bodies. I got to know some stunning women who believed lies about themselves and were made less effective as people because they could not see that they were beautiful.[16]

She also describes how evangelical Christian theology and predominantly male images of God compounded her self-hatred, and how profoundly dualistic anti-body world-views which Christianity bequeathed to her had very negative consequences:

> I believed that I loved myself too much. I indulged my appetite, I was too absorbed in myself. I was pandering to my body's desires. I believed this was why I had an eating disorder and the solution was to learn how to despise the flesh. It was to see my body as being the grotesque lump that it was. It was to hate greed and fat so much that I never indulged myself again.[17]

> Love my body? The very idea filled me with horror. Love
> this hideous lump of meat? Love the great white whale?
> How could I possibly love my enormous breasts, stretch-
> marked belly, outsize backside, flabby thighs and solid,
> thick feet? I was too ugly, too big, too pale, too fleshy, too
> bulky, too fat. Love my body? Sell drinks on sticks.[18]

Most of us hate ourselves, at some level. And as long as we
do, wellbeing will be only partial. For some of us Christian
theology exacerbates our self-hatred, for others, it alleviates it.
Sometimes Christian theology acts as a prophylactic to self-
hatred by offering unconditional acceptance of people just as
they are. But where this happens, it has to be remembered
that this is operational within a worldly context where the
capitalist performance mentality is the overwhelming force in
shaping our self-understanding. Any Christian engagement
with human wellbeing has to recognize this and devise
strategies for offering alternative value systems regarding
who human beings are and what we are worth, and why.
More of that in Chapter 3.

The irony of our capitalist context, however, is that health
has become just another commodity to be gained through a
combination of money, hard work and personal responsibility. Another job to be done; more SMART targets to be
striven for: healthy bones and teeth, healthy gums, healthy
hair, and fit, well-toned muscles. You can be a success at
getting healthy just as you can be a success at making money.
And you can be a failure too, of course. There are lots of
resources to help us, but they all come at a price: health clubs,
health insurance, cosmetic products and health magazines.
None of them can outwit the vagaries of genetic make-up,
accident, chance and luck, but there is a certain pleasure to be
gained in trying.

Sometimes it helps to step outside the system to see it for
what it is, though global capitalism is difficult to escape.
Interestingly, Eva Hoffman, a Polish-born writer who emigrated with her parents to Canada in the 1950s, makes observations about the socially constructed nature of concepts of

health and wellbeing in her book *Lost in Translation*. She describes the 'health culture' she encountered on arrival in a western performance-focused land:

> I'm confronted with the idea of health as effort. Run, swim, do aerobics, I am urged by every cultural loudspeaker. Run harder, run faster, run more every day. Keep moving, keep on the move. Expend energy. Build your body up so that it's as hard as a board, as muscular as an athlete's, as invulnerable as a steel machine . . . Once in a while, I go to a health club, that place where people, with a look of high seriousness on their faces, attach themselves to various contraptions and put successive parts of their bodies into strenuous motion. They are smooth, well-preserved, middle-class bodies for the most part – for class affects even how we get to look and age – and their healthy glow does credit to the machines and their own elaborate exertions. But I keep remembering the more indolent sensuousness that stood for health in my childhood, and I marvel at the eagerness to drive the body to the limit – as if one's flesh could be properly castigated that way, and the danger of passivity exorcised, like a deadly sin.[19]

Given all that has been said so far about our capitalist context, it would be surprising if our social understanding of health was anything other than highly individualistic and performance-oriented. In a sense there is nothing new in this – and, again, Wilson identifies this tendency in *Health is for People*: 'Our model of health is a medical one. It is also individualistic. We assume that health is an ideal state of human life in which an illness and handicap have been eliminated from each and every individual. We seek health by the prevention, diagnosis and treatment of disease in individual patients.'[20]

The concomitant of this individualistic understanding of health is that it is also mechanistic. If our vision for health is built upon the expectation that disease can and will be cured in each and every individual, then we had better feel pretty confident of the reliability of the ways and means of delivery. They need to be, among other things, definable and measurable. Wilson's challenge to this in 1976 was clear:

> The mechanistic approach to health as manifested in the technology of the National Health Service is now visibly inadequate. There is no way to health through the cure of illness. Indeed we can no longer maintain the old clinical distinction between 'wellness' and 'illness' upon which the Health Service is based. Rather than trying to reach health by understanding illness, we must first try to understand health, in the light of which we may be able to say something about being well or ill.[21]

Much has remained the same since Wilson first offered his critique of the assumptions underpinning modern medicine. Indeed, as technology has developed it is arguable that mechanistic approaches to health have been very much reinforced. But this is not the whole story. Interest in New Age spiritualities has grown quickly over the past few years. As Alex Wright documents in *Why Bother with Theology?*: 'The internet bookseller Amazon.co.uk lists ten categories of reading under its "Mind, Body, Spirit" section, each of which subdivides into numerous other – sometimes overlapping – sections and topics. The resulting range of choice is quite staggering.'[22] Two of the ten categories cited by Wright are health-related, 'complementary medicine' and 'self-help', highlighting the fact that interest in New Age ideas is often accompanied by, or originates in, a search for a holistic model of health and wellbeing. While these new holistic models of health and wellbeing are much less mechanistic than conventional medicine, there is much in them that remains highly individualistic. On the other hand, there are many exciting new developments in the politics of disability and in approaches to mental wellbeing (some of which will be addressed later in this book) which deploy so-called social models of disability and health, thereby challenging the individualism of past approaches to both these areas of service provision.

On a more popular level there is evidence that, among the relatively affluent at least, we are, as a society, embracing a more holistic approach to our health and wellbeing. On the other hand, these approaches do go hand in hand with 'money culture'. As Wright observes again:

Many newspapers and magazines nowadays (predominantly women's magazines, but increasingly publications targeting the expanding market for men's lifestyle and 'men's health') have regular articles on positive self-development. There is little preoccupation here with anything other than what are essentially ways of feeling better about oneself or of making one's immediate environment more attractive, frequently through the purchase of various kinds of goods.[23]

I decided to test this observation for myself by flicking through a few magazines which focus on health and wellbeing. I found this to be a most instructive exercise! The first thing to say is that these magazines are highly gender-specific: there are clearly men's magazines and women's magazines. These do not cover quite the same ground. *Men's Health*, for instance, is a magazine which includes coverage of health issues, but the title also functions as a euphemism for fashion and beauty. Women are allowed a whole separate genre for fashion and beauty, so health magazines are free to be less biased in this direction. For both genders, however, the boundary between 'health' and 'beauty/fashion' is blurred, as is the boundary between 'health' and 'fitness'. Likewise, since you clearly cannot address issues of health and wellbeing without talking about personal relationships and sexuality, sex constitutes a significant component, particularly in the men's magazines (women – heterosexual ones, that is – have this area of life well covered in 'fashion and beauty' publications).

Taking a typical issue of the magazine *Men's Health* (April 2002), we can analyse the contents as follows: of its 178 pages, 65 are taken up with adverts, 17 with news, views and updates on conventional health issues (with a medical bias), 19 pages are devoted to how to have better sex (with lots of complicated diagrams), 24 pages encourage increased fitness (how to grow muscle and work out effectively at the gym), 10 pages cover psychological issues, 6 pages focus on food, and 10 on fashion. The rest cover the usual miscellaneous items. I learned that chicken jalfrezi is the least fattening Indian takeaway option; that while cinnamon 'blasts bacteria', ginger 'nukes nausea'; that men (or some men at least) are as preoccupied with weight gain and weight loss as women, and that 9 per cent of the UK population are prone to panic attacks.

If I read many more of these magazines, I think I'd join that 9 per cent. In summary, the experience is both pleasurable and frustrating. They are a pleasurable read because each page is aesthetically pleasing, and never are we required to look at a body which is in any way unpleasant or unhealthy. Only fit ones (in both senses of the word) are on display. That's also, of course, what makes these magazines stressful to read. None of the bodies look like your real body, or the real bodies of anyone you know, so you wonder if you are inhabiting the right planet. The magazines offer a curious kind of hope, for health and wellbeing are clearly commodities alongside other commodities, so that significant aspects of health can apparently be bought, or brought about by design and hard work – de-stressing, looking better and getting fit, for instance. On the other hand, the processes by which such things might be brought about are presented, in the end, as incredibly confusing and complicated. You know that the only option is to read lots more until you've attained the holy grail of enlightenment. The subliminal question asked by these publications is something like, 'How can I be fit, well, beautiful and live for ever?' Deep down you know that the straightforward answer is that you can't. But by constantly asking the question, such magazines offer and reinforce the possibility that the impossible might, after all, be achievable. Stranger things have happened. To come back to our exploration of our political and social context, they are a triumph of the capitalism which fuels them, and by which they are fuelled. They both engender and satisfy desire. They are, perhaps, the middle-class equivalent of the salt that was once put into workers' beer to make them spend more of their hard-earned wages on it.

Cyborg Christians?

Let us recall where we have got to now in our exploration of health and wellbeing. I began with a reflection on Sarah's story, concluding that human wellbeing includes physical, psychological and spiritual elements, and that these are integrated and inseparable. Further, I suggested that relationships, identity and the negotiation of personal history are also key and overlapping factors. I then cast the exploratory net wider, assessing the cultural dynamics that shape our vision for health and wellbeing and define our personal hopes and expectations. I identified a cyborg ontology as a key to our contemporary self-understanding, and global capitalism as the dominant feature of our social and political backdrop. Finally, I have tried to explore some of the ways in which capitalism writes itself on to our bodies and minds, and works itself into our concepts of healthy individuals and communities. The next question is, what are the theological implications of living in the capitalist cyborg world as defined above? What options for health and wellbeing might Christians embrace in the midst of this fast-changing, multi-faceted secular world?

'Modern machines . . . are everywhere and they are invisible. Modern machinery is an irreverent upstart god, mocking the Father's ubiquity and spirituality.'[24] Cleverly and interestingly, Donna Haraway here hints at the theological challenge constituted by the changes she so brilliantly analyses. Is the cyborg world not straightforwardly an offence to God? Is it not a riotous celebration of all that is humanly created, to the exclusion of any recognition of the role and place of the divine creator of all things? Is it not the epitome of domination winning out over stewardship as humans interact with God's created world? Is not the physical and mental

ill-health and dis-ease which we see all around us in our
capitalist nations simply the logical outworking of what
evangelicals used to call, rather disarmingly, 'disobeying the
maker's instructions'?

If we believe that, then we might wish to embrace a 'back-
to-nature' ethic. In small ways, and very ironically, this ethic is
all around us in capitalist Britain. 'Organic' is assumed to be
better than 'inorganic', and 'natural' is better than 'artificial'. It
is seen in spiritualities which promise privileged access to an
'essential self', or which promise to put us in harmonious
touch with a singular life-force which underpins the universe.
There is a comforting back-to-basics ring to it all. Some take
this ethic much further than simply buying humanly created
products which are 'more natural than others', insisting also
on 'natural' fabrics and materials, and making some attempt
to grow their own food or to live self-sufficiently. But the
difficulties of achieving 'organic purity' within the capitalist
system are immense. For what is natural? What does it mean?
To be fair, for many purity is not the aim – they are simply trying to do the best they can and live as healthily as possible in a
thoroughly compromised context. But often the underlying
message is that there is something *wrong* with our engagement with technology, and something inherently *wrong* with
artificiality. How many times have you been with someone
who, answering the persistent ring of their mobile phone,
looks sheepish afterwards and mutters, 'I do hate mobiles,
don't you?'

But what is the theological alternative to back-to-nature
techno-resistance? Is there one? Interestingly, this debate has
already happened within the feminist movement. Where
some Christians might claim that our cyborg ontology
challenges the sovereignty of God, some feminists have dismissed it as the epitome of utilitarian patriarchal domination.
Haraway cites them as follows: 'American radical feminists
like Susan Griffin, Audre Lorde, and Adrienne Rich have . . .
perhaps restricted too much what we allow as a friendly body
and political language. They insist on the organic, opposing it
to the technological.'[25] Indeed, she suggests this tendency

goes beyond feminist thinking to progressive politics in general: 'the analytic resources developed by progressives have insisted on the necessary domination of technics and recalled us to an imagined organic body to integrate our resistance'.[26] Haraway's great contribution to this debate is her refusal to allow that the organic and the technological have to be set up in opposition to one another. Most importantly, she raises the spectre of an ethical engagement with a cyborg ontology which does not involve either uncritical acquiescence or total resistance:

> There are several consequences to taking seriously the imagery of cyborgs as other than our enemies. Our bodies, ourselves; bodies are maps of power and identity. Cyborgs are no exception. A cyborg body is not innocent; it was not born in a garden; it does not seek unitary identity and so generate antagonistic dualisms without end (or until the world ends); it takes irony for granted . . . Intense pleasure in skill, machine skill, ceases to be a sin, but an aspect of embodiment. The machine is not an *it* to be animated, worshipped, and dominated. The machine is us, our processes, an aspect of our embodiment. We can be responsible for machines; *they* do not dominate or threaten us. We are responsible for boundaries; we are they.[27] (italics hers)

This takes a bit of explaining. Haraway is starting from a position of resistance to the dualistic world-view which has dominated western modes of thinking. We are familiar with such dualisms as critiqued by feminist theologians: the split between self/other, mind/body, culture/nature, male/female, civilized/primitive, reality/appearance, whole/part, maker/made, active/passive, black/white, right/wrong, truth/illusion, total/partial, God/man (to name but a few!). It is this dualism which has facilitated and justified the domination of the lower order in each case (people of colour, women, the body, etc.), and in breaking down the formerly clean distinctions which have structured the western self, many positive possibilities for justice have resulted.

Haraway is simply arguing that the old dualism which separated body from spirit and man from woman has also separated human from animal and human from machine. Could it be, she suggests, that the same positive possibilities for justice might be pursued in embracing the breakdown of the distinction between the organic and the technological?

In other words, what were once clear boundaries between the 'organic' and the 'technological', the 'natural' and the 'artificial', are now no longer given. They are negotiable. Whatever boundaries we decide upon we will also be held responsible for. We shift from the realm of the 'natural' to the realm of the political and the ethical. The aim is not to replace the rigid rules and restrictions associated with our old dualistic world-view with 'anything goes'. Quite the opposite: as Haraway puts it, 'This . . . is an argument for *pleasure* in the confusion of boundaries and for *responsibility* in their construction.'[28] And, 'my cyborg myth is about transgressed boundaries, potent fusions, and dangerous possibilities which progressive people might explore as one part of needed political work.'[29]

Whether we like her myth or not, what is clear is that we cannot go back, even if we wanted to, and most of us would not want to. The only way is forward, and the only credible theo-ethical position must be one of being savvy about power and its abuses, using the potential of our cyborg ontology to forge tools for transforming our world into a place where health and wellbeing are at least a possibility. Andrew Solomon agrees, and begins to sketch out for us a manifesto for change that will be taken up in more detail later in this book:

> Few of us want to, or can, give up modernity of thought any more than we want to give up modernity of material existence. But we must start doing small things now to lower the level of socio-emotional pollution. We must look for faith (in anything: God or the self or other people or politics or beauty or just about anything else) and structure. We must help the disenfranchised whose suffering undermines

so much of the world's joy – for the sake both of those huddled masses and of the privileged people who lack profound motivation in their own lives. We must practise the business of love, and we must teach it too. We must ameliorate the circumstances that conduce to our terrifyingly high levels of stress. We must hold out against violence, and perhaps against its representations. This is not a sentimental proposal; it is as urgent as the cry to save the rain forest.[30]

And so a programme of ethical and theological endeavour is beginning to emerge from our assessment of cyborg culture. The opposite of wellbeing is not illness, but dis-ease, in the sense of unease – being ill-at-ease with ourselves. Wellbeing is not the result of 'cure' but of the incremental building of networks of relationships and human connection, self-esteem, self-belief, purpose, meaning, value and good relationships. These tasks must be undertaken corporately, as well as individually. Health and wellbeing are not commodities to be bought, as we are popularly encouraged to believe; they are the fruits, for individuals and communities, of living well. Our capitalist cyborg context calls forth from us a new kind of theological engagement. Nostalgia is not enough. We can no longer live as though we were stable selves, in natural bodies, with essential souls, worshipping an unchanging God. We need instead a religious identity that embraces the complexity of our shifting selves and of our fast-changing world.

2

SICK?

He had no form or majesty that we should look at him, nothing in his appearance that we should desire him. He was despised and rejected by others; a man of suffering and acquainted with infirmity; and as one from whom others hide their faces he was despised, and we held him of no account . . . like a lamb that is led to the slaughter, and like a sheep that before its shearers is silent, so he did not open his mouth. By a perversion of justice he was taken away. Who could have imagined his future?

(Isaiah 53)

Lent, Holy Week, Easter 2001 – an odyssey of sickness and death. Who will forget the heavy grey-black smoke of burning carcasses as cattle, diseased and healthy, smouldered in trenches? Or the pictures of the cadavers before they were burned: stiff yet bloated, legs in the air in a final gesture of victimhood. The transport of despair from death to incineration was either forklift truck (the force-multiplier of the inanimate) or crane, from which bodies dangled in giant metal grippers reminiscent of that nameless game at the fairground – perhaps a fitting symbol for these beasts of a random and luckless fate.

Ungainly. Undignified. Ugly. These were the once-living beings which, though most of us avoided it most of the time, we could have related to, now dead and objectified by the media and by us as consumers of it. Their sorry end a direct result of desperate human policies which seemed most of the time to be based on little more than guesswork: shots, literally, in the dark as we attempted to burn our way out of a plague; slaughter our way beyond a curse – foot-and-mouth disease. FMD. Life felt medieval as we resorted to near superstition:

ringing church bells at midday, wading through disinfectant. Setting up border-crossings of straw.

Then the television camera lens roved more widely, exploring the underlying causes of the spread of this disease. Suddenly we were inside an abattoir, watching carcasses being sliced deftly, meat that you expected to be red with blood strangely dry and almost black in colour, the commentary repeating words which themselves created images of horror: slaughter; spinal cord; offal. Then finally, worst of all, we were in that hell-hole warehouse in Leicestershire with piles of chicken body-parts, yellow with the dye which marks them out as unfit for human consumption, decomposing and apparently, before the scam was foiled, on their way back into the human food chain.

At sixteen I joined Student Community Action at my school, volunteering each week with half a dozen others to help run the local Gateway Club for adults with learning disabilities. At first this felt to me like a strange and alien world. I struggled with strong emotional and physical reactions to this experience which, significantly, I never spoke of at the time. Regardless of how hungry I was when I left school in the minibus, once I arrived at the club my appetite diminished – to be replaced by a mild, barely perceptible, nausea. There were, of course, rational reasons for this. The whole place smelt very strongly of the tea that we distributed to the club members from huge battered metal teapots. I dislike tea and cannot drink it. The food consisted, week after week, of cheese and salad cream sandwiches and angel cake, neither of which I would eat given the choice. But my physical reactions were about more than that, though I failed to analyse at the time exactly what was going on.

About five years later, the feeling returned. This time it stayed with me for several months. The cause? Falling in love with another woman, and embarking on a lesbian relationship. The inability to eat properly lasted for the best part of a year, and when I forget that this ever happened, I need only to flip back the pages of the photo album to see a rather diminutive me. This was not an eating disorder. It was shame.

Entirely unexpected and, worse, inexplicable for one who had never had an intellectual or moral or theological problem with same-sex relationships. Coupled with that was the realization that suddenly I had become one of a category of people who cause in others feelings of revulsion and disgust. I cannot explain to anyone who hasn't experienced it what that feels like.

And so I learned how congealed social values write themselves on and in our own individual bodies in a very powerful way. And that this is the case, crucially, *whatever we believe about the rights or wrongs of those social values*. Our intellectual assent or dissent is irrelevant, at least at first, in the face of the power of the body politic.

Later still I heard survivors of abuse talk about the physical effects of that abuse; the inexplicable feelings of shame for that which was not their fault, and I knew what level this was working at. The corporate body says that this is defilement – impurity, just as the corporate body politic says that those with a learning disability are somehow beyond the boundary of what it means to be human, and that the queer muck up male/female dualities, so need to be expunged. This is all part of the same picture.

And it's a picture which I subsequently got sociological and philosophical help with. I learned from Julia Kristeva that there is a category of stuff which is considered neither subject nor object, but abject. 'It is not', she says, 'lack of cleanliness or health that causes abjection but what disturbs identity, system, order. What does not respect borders, positions, rules. The in-between, the ambiguous, the composite.'[1] The loathsome, she says, is that which disobeys classification and does not respect boundaries. So the aspects of human physicality which we traditionally find repulsive – blood, saliva, excreta, urine, semen – are deemed to be 'marginal stuff', because in issuing forth they have *traversed the boundary* of the body. And in *Purity and Danger*,[2] Mary Douglas puts forward her now famous definition of dirt as 'matter out of place'. That which is constructed by society as 'dirty' or 'polluted' is not so because of any intrinsic qualities of its own, but is a relative concept.

Shoes are not dirty in themselves, but they are if you put them on the kitchen table. If the chicken parts were on their way to the incinerator, we wouldn't have so much of a problem with them. What was repulsive was the fact we were told they were on their way into chicken pies that we might just eat. Little different, in fact, from eating shit. They were meant for waste, but were becoming food again.

'My God, my God, why have you forsaken me? And are so far from my cry and from the words of my distress? O my God, I cry in the daytime, but you do not answer; by night as well, but I find no rest . . . I am a worm and no man, scorned by all and despised by the people' (Psalm 22).

Let's return to the odyssey of Holy Week and Easter. There is much in the passion narrative to ponder on. It's all about physicality and body fluids. Jesus, at various points in the story, is anointed with perfume; kissed by his betrayer. He weeps over Jerusalem and sweats in Gethsemane. He shares food and wine and washes feet. He is spat upon by soldiers, beaten until he bleeds, slapped round the face and crowned with thorns. He is taken *outside of the city boundary* to be crucified, is given sour wine on a hyssop stem to drink at the point of death, and after death his side is pierced so that blood and water can flow.

This is a brutally embodied story of Christ's humanity. And is it not the story of the greatest creative and life-changing boundary transgression that ever happened: that between the divine and human? Hardly surprising, if that's the case, that the Good Friday story is the repulsive bit which we find hard to tell and hard to hear. As many have said, we find it easier to skip to Easter Day, when all is washed and clean again. Better still, skip straight to the ascension so we can forget about bodies altogether – and forget that this disgusting thing ever happened. God's back in his heaven, we're still bound to earth, and the incarnation is mere theological abstraction.

Exploring sickness

Inclusion is a pattern of health, *exclusion* a pattern of death (the leper). In social terms a society may 'kill' (may treat in a way which spells death for) those of whom it disapproves, those whom it fears, those by whom it feels itself threatened. So society excludes (kills, sometimes literally) either by its attitudes, by segregation, institutionalisation or execution, the bad, the mad, the black, the widow, the leper, the aged, the underprivileged, the mentally subnormal, the rebel and the dying. This exclusive pattern of dealing with 'pollution' results in a 'safe' and sanitated society, but not a healthy society.[3]

This chapter is about the dynamics of sickness – individual experiences of it, and its social symbolism. Central to the argument is a recognition that facing up to sickness is about facing up to that which repels us, and a conviction that there is a creative space afforded by transgression of the boundary between the sick and the well which can be life-giving, even in death. My perspective is that while we struggle towards a policy of promoting good health for all, we do this against a corporate psychological background of denial. Each and every one of us is encouraged to think that illness, impairment, disability and death are exceptional and, more importantly, that they will never happen to us. In many cases, therefore, these things make us profoundly uncomfortable. They may even disgust us. The question then is, how can all citizens, and especially those who temporarily enjoy good health, be encouraged to participate in health care agendas when we are simultaneously deeply psychologically invested in the notion that such participation is – except as an altruistic act of charity – irrelevant to us?

If we lived in ancient Greece, many of us would meet a very unpleasant end. Once a year, a selection of slaves, foreigners, criminals, people with disabilities, and others who were in some way different, were rounded up. For a while they were very well treated, then, on a special festival, they were paraded round the city; the conflicts and difficulties of the community were symbolically placed upon them, and they were then killed, their bodies burned and the ashes thrown into the sea or a river.

The ceremony took place on the outskirts of the city. This symbolized the fact that conflicts and problems were being taken from within the community and disposed of. Hence the need to use those who were both *part of* the community and *not part of it*: those who belonged to the community, but, because of their difference, were also set apart. Only such marginal people were in a position to take problems away from the community. The name for this was *pharmakos* – scapegoating. Note the common root with *pharmacist*. Both were thought to bring healing. There are indications of this taking place in other cultures too, not least in Ancient Israel. The dictionary definition of 'scapegoat' is, 'a goat on which, once a year, the Jewish High Priest laid symbolically the sins of the people, and which was then allowed to escape into the wilderness. Or, any animal used in like manner: one who is made to bear the misdeeds of another.'[4]

Literal scapegoating may be confined to history and to ancient societies, but as Michael Wilson hints (see p. 46), it would be a mistake to think that the social dynamics of scapegoating have lost their resonance in our postmodern context. Though some of the language that he used in the 1970s could not comfortably be used now, Wilson helps us to see that the scapegoat analogy is a useful key to understanding the perplexing dynamics of health and illness that operate in our society. Especially if we take into account the psychological and emotional functioning of the concept, alongside the social and political. Kat Duff points out:

In blaming the sick – or the poor, or anyone else who has met with misfortune and injustice – scapegoaters feel lighter, freer, stronger, and safer from the afflictions of life, relieved of the burden of their own fears, mistakes, misgivings. The scapegoated, on the other hand, feel inferior, heavy, guilty, and vulnerable, for they are burdened with the unanswered questions, the shame and shadow of the collective. Whilst we all partake of both sides of this dynamic at various points and places in our lives, those primarily identified with the scapegoat role acknowledge and suffer the wounds we all share, and come to manifest the symptoms: ruptures of psyche and body.[5]

Let us explore in more detail the dynamics of scapegoating within the context of our ongoing discussion about health and wellbeing. What are the experiences, and who are the people, we feel it necessary to expunge and exclude in order to feel 'lighter, freer, stronger, and safer from the afflictions of life'? I suggest three categories: old age and the elderly, death and those who are dying, disease and those who are sick.

When I was seven or eight years old the garden of our house and the churchyard next to it (which provided a useful extension to our play territory) backed on to the grounds of a large residential home for elderly people. Or 'old people's home' as we used to call it. At least that's what, at some point, I was told it was. I remember it as a large grey building set in spacious grounds, very unimaginatively landscaped. The gardens were flat and almost all set to lawn with a tall, wide, always immaculately kept privet hedge all round the perimeter, growing right up to the wall. My friends and I would often play on the wall, climbing up it and running along it. We would peer at the building and strain our eyes to see inside. But it was too far away, and there rarely seemed to be any sign of life. Occasionally, an old woman would come to the window and signal to us, none too politely, to go away. This was both terrifying and exhilarating. With hindsight, I remember this as not simply fear of the consequences of getting into trouble. It was more than that. Seeing the old woman was terrifying because the inhabitants had somehow gone through a complete 'othering' process in our young minds. I've a feeling we had been told to 'keep away from there', presumably to give the residents peace and quiet. But we had interpreted this imperative to 'keep away' as a sign of danger within. Because the residents were 'very old' and were, for the most part, hidden away, they had become hardly human in our seven-year-old minds. We had made up stories about the mysterious inhabitants inside this anonymous-looking building – stories of witches and ogres – so when the shaking fist appeared at the window, this was confirmation to our childish sensibilities that our fantasies were true.

But to arouse a response from behind those walls was also exhilarating because, ultimately, we felt safe – powerful even. As long as we kept to our side of the wall, all was well. Interestingly, while we were quite happy to trespass in the churchyard, we never crossed the wall and hedge into the grounds of the old people's home. We could easily have jumped into the grounds, though to get out again would have presented some logistical difficulties given the thickness and height of the hedge in front of the wall. But we were young and agile and all good climbers, and this was ordinarily the kind of challenge we would enjoy. But in this case, speaking for myself at least, I feared that if I crossed that boundary I would be somehow captured – sucked into the land of the old and never relinquished.

Later, we moved to a town in a rural area with very few leisure facilities for young people. No swimming pool, no cinema, no sports facilities. When I became enthusiastic about tennis, there were few options for practice outside of school. Eventually, though, by some concession, my best friend and I were permitted to use the tennis court at the small local hospital. The difficulty was that we had to collect the key to the court from *inside* the building.

Many people who are unfamiliar with hospitals have a dread of them, and my friend and I were no exceptions. We both hated it so much that we would take it in turns to collect the key, which was kept behind the nurses' desk on the geriatric ward. I was old enough by then to feel ashamed of the feelings I had whenever it was my turn. I sensed that it was bad to feel dread and embarrassment on entering that place, and fought against the nausea that hit the back of my throat at the familiar smell of urine and disinfectant. I knew that the presences huddled on high chairs by the beds – and those bodies lying in bed so frail that they seemed barely existent – were human beings just like me. I knew that it was rude to stare, but also rude to ignore the eyes that caught mine as I skipped down the corridor, suddenly and newly aware of my youth and mobility. There was always a lot going on behind my friendly smile and nonchalant chat with whichever nurses were on duty. But most of all, there was an overwhelming desire to be out of there – as quickly as possible.

And yet all of us will grow old, unless we die first. And most of us, as children, have been close to older people through our family and community networks. I certainly encountered, through church, lots of elderly people from a very early age. Yet this experiential familiarity was obviously not educationally forceful enough to outwit the influence of other social forces – powerful social forces that despise old age and the infirmity that often, eventually, accompanies it.

In our exploration of the meaning of health, I mentioned that the perceived proximity to death affects our perceptions of old age. In our society there is a special level of horror reserved for death and therefore for those who are known imminently to be facing it.

Philosopher Julia Kristeva, mentioned in my opening reflection, effectively sums up what is at stake:

> Refuse and corpses *show me* what I permanently thrust aside in order to live. These bodily fluids, this defilement, this shit are what life withstands, hardly and with difficulty, on the part of death. There, I am at the border of my condition as a living being. My body extricates itself, as being alive, from that border. Such wastes drop so that I might live, until, from loss to loss, nothing remains in me and my entire body falls beyond the limit – *cadere*, cadaver.[6] (italics hers)

How do we, as a society, cope with the embodiment of death? Some years ago I heard the following story on *The World at One* while eating my lunch:

Great Eastern Railways confirmed that up to 20 drivers had been told to drive their packed trains over the body of a young woman as it lay for four hours on the Shenfield to Southend line, in Essex. The woman, aged 28, is believed to have committed suicide on the track at five in the morning and her body was left on the rails until nine, in the interests of rush-hour travellers.

The remains of my cheese on toast went straight in the bin.

The commentary and ensuing debate were all about the privatization of public services and the resulting all-consuming need and desire to maximize profit: about how in the non-caring, non-sharing 1990s (as it was then) this pressure had become so intense that it had apparently overridden even the human ethical imperative to treat 'the dead' with respect and dignity. But the commentary didn't touch, for me, what was really at stake in all this. It felt all too distant; too theoretical. There was a marked dissonance between the rationality of the discussion and the intensity of my emotional (and physical) reaction to the story. I listened hard, waiting for a glimmer of enlightenment which would help me make sense of what was really going on. Something important was missing.

The day before, I had been at a funeral. A beautiful funeral, if that's the right word. Before this funeral I had never seen a dead body, never even questioned why we say 'dead body' and not 'dead person' or 'the body of someone who has died'. Central to this funeral was the body of the woman who had died, held in an open coffin. This was carried into the church one hour before the funeral began so that mourners could keep vigil – say goodbye to her. The coffin was carried by loved-ones. They carried it with a kind of concentrated tenderness.

It was intensely and unbearably moving to watch as the mourners, one by one, approached the coffin. Reflected in each face were traces of memories of a life lived and now over. The woman was powerfully present through her bodily self. She was written all over the faces of those who beheld her. I didn't know her well, but I felt I had more insight into the person that she was by the end of the funeral than I did at the beginning. Rare in my experience of funerals.

The thought of a dead woman having a tarpaulin thrown over her by a railway official as though her body was of no consequence or significance represented a monstrous contrast to the treatment of 'body' at this funeral. Yet in the midst of these two experiences, I was suddenly aware that my unease with the Radio 4 news story sprang from a deep ambivalence. Espousing the need for Christians to value the body and embodiment was a familiar part of my feminist theological repertoire. But I suddenly realized that I had always, until that point, assumed bodies to be live entities. But bodies can be dead too – although a host of social forces conspire to prevent us from facing this self-evident fact. To value bodies as dead entities posed a new challenge, and suddenly a part of me wanted to revert to old-fashioned dualistic cosmologies. Better not to value dead bodies. Better not even to think about them. Better to treat them in a purely functional way. But that is exactly what the railway company did. Presumably they thought, 'The woman is dead, so what does it matter how we treat her body?' That funeral led me to realize, however, that nothing matters more. In life and death, bodies are and do matter.

Our social death taboo affects much more than just our attitude to people's bodies in death, and to death itself. It influences other aspects of our 'health' service, as Michael Wilson points out:

> Many social attitudes and much behaviour in hospital can only be explained on the assumption that 'death is the worst thing that can happen to a man' [sic]. We note a reluctance to speak about death or to tell patients about a fatal prognosis, the withdrawal of attention from patients for whom doctors can do no more, pointless resuscitation and prolongation of life, the allocation of funds and staff to Intensive Treatment Units and the impoverishment of hospitals concerned with care, all this behaviour is rooted in our present social 'taboo' of death. We are a death-fearing

society, and the practice of medicine and nursing is influenced by such social fears and expectations.[7]

Gillian Rose, who died of cancer in the late 1990s, explores in her brilliant philosophical autobiography, *Love's Work*, the attitudes to death that she encountered during the course of her cancer treatment. She bears out Wilson's analysis when she says, 'Surgeons are not qualified for the one thing with which they deal: life. For they do not understand, as part of their profession, "death", in the non-medical sense, nor therefore "life" in the meaningful sense, inclusive of death. When they fail to "cure", according to their own lights, they deal out death.'[8]

This discussion began with the recognition of scapegoating as a useful analogy for our social attitudes towards old age, sickness and death. We have seen that attitudes to all three are inextricably linked. So far, we have explored the overlap between old age and death, but in the process of focusing on death, we have been drawn inevitably into discussions about sickness. In her book *Illness As Metaphor*, Susan Sontag suggests that our attitudes to cancer are inevitably bound up with our attitudes to death: 'All this lying to and by cancer patients is a measure of how much harder it has become in advanced industrial societies to come to terms with death. As death is now an offensively meaningless event, so that disease widely considered a synonym for death is experienced as something to hide.'[9] But there is much else about sickness, physical and mental, which our society construes as horrifying, making illness something to be excluded from our socially sanctioned purview and imagination.

Written out of her experience of Chronic Fatigue Syndrome (CFS), Kat Duff's *The Alchemy of Illness* highlights an issue about physical sickness that I raised in my introduction. It must be time-limited to be contained within the 'manageable' or 'socially acceptable' (Aren't you better yet?). Long-term, indefinable illnesses like CFS (or ME) cause horror because they have no definable end. They make us uneasy: 'I have come to realize that many people are deeply disturbed by the fact of my continuing illness; they want to help but also need to reassure themselves that disasters can be avoided and, if necessary, easily remedied.'[10]

Long-term illness which cannot be explained or cured symbolizes that which our scientific and rationalist society has sought to overcome: the chaotic, the uncontrollable, the mysterious. Needless to say, the persistence and power of these social influences can have a devastating impact on individuals who are ill: 'When pain and disability prove to be intractable, and savings disappear, marriages flounder, and confidence is shattered, the old answers just do not work anymore. We feel betrayed by the promises of cures that can be found in almost every magazine, and forsaken by doctors, family, and friends who cannot really help, but keep suggesting another treatment.'[11]

In her work on illness (particularly AIDS) as metaphor, Susan Sontag steers us through the complex world of the social construction of illness, making it clear that not all illnesses are equally feared, or feared for the same reasons. She suggests that the proximity and likelihood of death is not the only determinant of the levels of dread and horror associated with disease. As she explains, for instance:

Cancer is more feared than heart disease, although someone who has had a coronary is more likely to die of heart disease in the next few years than someone who has cancer is likely to die of cancer. A heart attack is an event but it does not give someone a new identity, turning the patient into one of 'them'. It is not transforming, except in the sense of a transformation into something better: inspired by fear, the cardiac patient acquires good habits of exercise and diet, starts to lead a more prudent, healthier life. And it is often thought to produce, if only because it can be instantaneous, an easy death.[12]

And,

while cholera killed fewer people in Western Europe in the

nineteenth century than smallpox did, it was more feared, because of the suddenness with which it struck and the indignity of the symptoms: fulminant diarrhea and vomiting, whose result anticipated the horror of post-mortem decomposition.

. . . Polio's effects could be horrifying – it withered the body – but it did not mark or rot the flesh: it was not repulsive. Further, polio affected the body only, though that may seem ruin enough, not the face. The relatively appropriate, unmetaphorical reaction to polio owes much to the privileged status of the face, so determining of our evaluation of physical beauty and of physical ruin.[13]

Interestingly, this is borne out in contemporary life too. Saving Faces is a charity founded to raise money for research into oral and facial cancers. The organization arranged an art exhibition with the same title at the National Portrait Gallery featuring those whose faces have been changed in the course of facial reconstruction after the removal of cancerous tumours. The artist, Mark Gilbert, chronicled patients' progress before, during and after surgery. In an article in the *Guardian*, journalist Libby Brooks points out that these cancers have few advocates, and quotes the founder of Saving Faces as saying, 'It's a very isolating, very lonely disease . . .' Brooks also says, 'In the period during which cancers affecting the head and neck received £190,000 from research bodies, breast cancer received £12m.'[14]

By coincidence, in the very same issue of the *Guardian*, I came across another story highlighting our socially constructed attitude of repulsion to facial disfigurement. Under the title 'The Hidden Horrors', Peter Lennon reported on a new movie, *The Officers' Ward*, based on a novel by Marc Dougain:

One day about seven years ago, Marc Dougain . . . came across a photograph of his grandfather taken on the eve of the first world war. It was profoundly shocking because this was a picture of a handsome young man looking with an assured and expectant air into the future; Dougain had only known his grandfather as a man with half his face blown away, mouth, cheek and nose gouged out by a shell in the first week of hostilities. Possessed by an over-whelming desire to understand how *someone rendered so repulsive to society goes on living*, Dougain took leave and wrote furiously for 15 days.[15] (italics mine)

For those of us with sight, looking at and into the face is a crucial way of getting to know another human being. The face is a key signifier of identity. We can understand society's particular discomfort with facial disfigurement if we revisit the insights of Kristeva, that what causes abjection is that which disturbs identity, system, order.

A complex combination of factors is therefore at work in our social, historically located responses to physical sickness. There is the horror of symptoms which bring us face to face with abjection (or which simply excite the imagined possi-bility of an encounter with abjection) – the thought, for instance, of boundary-transgressing bodily fluids or of rotting and decomposition; there is the fear of chaos and of losing control of one's life; and there is the fear of loss or transforma-tion of identity – the possibility that through our sickness we become someone else, someone 'other'. As Kat Duff puts it, 'We do not dip our feet into the waters of illness; we are fully immersed in them, as if pulled under by a relentless under-tow. As we become sick, sickness becomes us and redefines us, so we say we are not ourselves anymore.'[16]

In an observation which brings us back to the heart of our ongoing discussion of the analogy of the scapegoat, Sontag says:

Any disease that is treated as a mystery and acutely enough feared will be felt to be morally, if not literally, contagious. Thus, a surprisingly large number of people with cancer find themselves being shunned by relatives and by members of their household, as if cancer, like TB, were an infectious disease. Contact with someone afflicted with a disease regarded as a mysterious malevolency inevitably feels like a trespass; worse, like the violation of a taboo.[17]

This phenomenon of 'moral contagion' was manifested most recently through socio-political reactions to the emergence of the HIV virus. Remember the tabloid fulminations in the late 1980s about a 'killer plague' to which everyone was vulnerable? Remember the discussions among right-wingers as to whether all those who were HIV-positive shouldn't just be rounded up and incarcerated? Remember the recriminations of those who maintained that those with AIDS-related illnesses were drowning in a moral cesspool of their own making? Remember the distinction that was made between 'innocent victims' (those infected through transfusions of blood products), and 'the others', deemed to have only themselves to blame because they were infected through sexual activity?

These early responses to HIV and AIDS may appear to be exceptional examples of victim-blaming. But I would argue that they are simply a more extreme form of a tendency that is present in our responses as a society to sickness in general. Remember the scapegoat dynamic explored earlier: the scapegoated need to be made to feel 'inferior, heavy, guilty, and vulnerable' in order for the scapegoaters to feel 'lighter, freer, stronger, and safer from the afflictions of life'.[18] In order for the well to feel that they are invulnerable to sickness, the sick must be held – at some level – to be personally responsible and blameworthy for their own condition. Sontag's work bears this out. She speaks of the evolution of the concept of what has become known as 'the cancer personality'. The myth is that certain people are prone to contracting cancer because of their inability to express their feelings openly: 'Both the myth about TB and the current myth about cancer propose that one is responsible for one's disease . . . there is mostly shame attached to a disease thought to stem from the repression of emotion.'[19] And elsewhere she maintains that 'the cancer personality is regarded more simply, and with condescension, as one of life's losers'.[20]

Research has shown that emotional distress has an impact on the body's ability to resist disease. This is as one would expect given the inter-relationship of the physical and the psychological. But, as Sontag says, 'the hypothesis that distress can affect immunological responsiveness (and, in some circumstances, lower immunity to disease) is hardly the same as – or constitutes evidence for – the view that emotions cause diseases, much less for the belief that specific emotions can produce specific diseases.'[21] She also points out that, 'The fantasy that a happy state of mind would fend off disease probably flourished for all infectious diseases, before the nature of infection was understood. Theories that diseases are caused by mental states and can be cured by will power are always an index of how much is not understood about the physical terrain of a disease.'[22]

CFS or ME is a classic contemporary example of what Sontag is saying here. Little is know about its cause, and even less about how to treat it. There was a time when many doctors denied that it existed at all, preferring to suggest that those who were sick were simply imagining their illness, and therefore were in need of psychiatric help. For Kat Duff, the following insight followed her experiences of CFS, when she was made to feel that, 'Sickness . . . is not only a breakdown of normal health but also a personal failure, which explains why so many sick people feel so guilty and ashamed.'[23] She also says, 'patients with maladies deemed organic are treated respectfully, and those with so-called mental problems are dismissed with derision. But the experience of illness defies that dichotomy, insisting that body and psyche are inseparable.'[24]

This value system extends to mental health issues too. If a mental state is deemed to have an 'organic' or 'physical' cause, we feel much better about it. A perspective which Andrew Solomon challenges as follows:

The relief people express when a doctor says the depression is 'chemical' is predicated on a belief that there is an integral self that exists across time, and on a fictional divide between the fully occasioned sorrow and the utterly random one. The word *chemical* seems to assuage the feelings of responsibility people have for the stressed-out discontent of not liking their jobs, worrying about getting old, failing at love, hating their families. There is a pleasant freedom from guilt that has been attached to *chemical*. If your brain is predisposed to depression, you need not blame yourself for it. Well, blame yourself or evolution, but remember that blame itself can be understood as a chemical process, and that happiness, too, is chemical. Chemistry and biology are not matters that impinge on the 'real' self; depression cannot be separated from the person it affects. Treatment does not alleviate a disruption of identity, bringing you back to some kind of normality; it readjusts a multifarious identity, changing in some small degree who you are.[25]

It is interesting that he alludes, in his analysis, to the identity-disrupting potential of depression. He suggests that in the face of this we work towards a more sophisticated model of the self as multifarious, rather than assuming a singular 'essential' self which remains unchanged across time. A discussion of the merits of such a change in self-concept is beyond our current discussion, but it underlines again the point that identity disruption is a key factor in our discomfort with illness, both physical and mental.

Once we used to segregate those with mental illnesses and those with learning disabilities in large hospitals – the so-called lunatic asylums. The heritage of these is inscribed on the physical and psychological landscape of many of our major towns and cities. Even to utter the name of these hospitals – most of which have significance only locally – is to foster dread. The complicating factor, of course, is that you didn't necessarily need to be ill or to have a disability to end up with a life sentence in one. Certain behaviour by members of certain social classes was contained by extending the definition of madness to warrant incarceration in such asylums. Proof enough, perhaps, of Wilson's suggestion that society kills (metaphorically speaking) those of whom it disapproves, this time by deeming them to be ill. Apparently a small number of the 'elderly mentally frail' in the town where I live, Malvern, are those who were resettled some years ago from the large psychiatric hospital on the edge of Worcester. According to one local mental health social worker who supports them, some of the women were there for no other reason than having been made pregnant by their bosses as young girls in domestic service. Which returns us to a consideration of who we blame and who we exclude, and for what reasons.

Modern mental health policy focuses on offering appropriate support in the community to those with mental health needs – as will be explored later. But the fact remains that our corporately generated horror of what used to be called madness and insanity leaves 'the community' with a terrifically strong in-built stigma against those with acute mental health needs. This stigma is coupled with a predominant social silence about mental health issues in general, even though a significant proportion of us are likely to experience mental ill-health severe enough to warrant medical treatment at some point in our lives: 'Mental health problems are common: currently one in seven adults experiences a mental health problem and it is estimated that one in four people will have a mental health problem in the course of a year. The most common problems are anxiety and depression – 77 in 1,000 people at any one time experience symptoms.'[26]

In the context of our current discussion, plans to reform the 1983 Mental Health Act constitute an interesting case study. The Church of England Board for Social Responsibility has critiqued these plans in some depth, not least through a one-day conference in February 2001 entitled 'Personality Disorder and Human Worth'. Theologian Nicholas Sagovsky clearly laid out what was at stake:

> The Government has now brought forward its policy proposals in *Reforming the Mental Health Act*, a White Paper in two parts ... At the heart of the new framework is an expansion of powers to detain, treat and care for patients who are

thought to be a danger to themselves and to others. Such detention would be based on a very broad definition of 'mental disorder' which does not distinguish between personality disorder and mental illness.

. . . The White Paper also refers, without definition, to 'severe personality disorder'. The problem of defining and identifying 'personality disorder' is a major issue in the whole discussion of 'high risk patients' . . . It is generally agreed to be a step forward from 'psychopathy', and it is widely agreed that as a working description of the hypothetical cause for certain sorts of human behaviour it is extremely useful. It is also recognised that it is frequently used as a kind of 'catch-all' description for people who are difficult and unrewarding to treat and that it may at times have little more meaning than 'nasty and unco-operative'.[27]

Here we see the deliberate construction of a new category of people with a disorder known as DSPD (Dangerous and Severe Personality Disorder). These people are deemed untreatable, and can be preventively detained (though unconvicted of any crimes) on the grounds that there is a possibility that they may cause harm to themselves or others. Unsurprisingly, these proposals have excited much criticism, not least from some of the psychiatrists who will be called upon to pronounce the diagnosis upon which decisions about people's freedom will rest. One particularly passionate critic of the plans is Bob Johnson, a psychiatrist formerly of the Parkhurst Special Unit, who says this: 'The label "personality disorder" is coming to resemble that of "leper" in the Middle Ages. How would you react if the equivalent of a leper colony was proposed today? And if this were happening in our society, even if surreptitiously, what would you do?'[28]

Tabloid 'monsters' and 'psychopaths' are just one of our present-day social pollutants, presented as dangerous and chaotic, an ever-present and ominous threat to decent civilized people. Perhaps DSPD is the more elegant terminology of the broadsheets, a scientifically more contained and defined social problem. But, according to Bob Johnson, 'established psychiatry, at least as expressed in the current psychiatric "bible" (the DSM-IV), has not the least idea where personality disorder comes from'.[29]

The treatment of those with acute mental health needs, who may be a danger to others or (much more likely) to themselves, is a complex and difficult issue. But there is a real danger that DSPD may evolve into just another category of 'the sick' – a category from which the rest of us can disassociate ourselves in order to define ourselves as well and normal.

Transgressing boundaries

There is, perhaps rightly so, an invisible rope that separates the sick from the well, so that each is repelled by the other, like magnets reversed. The well venture forth to accomplish great deeds in the world, while the sick turn back onto themselves and commune with the dead; neither can face the other very comfortably, without intrusions of envy, resentment, fear, or horror. Frankly, from the viewpoint of illness, healthy people seem ridiculous, even a touch dangerous, in their blinded busyness, marching like soldiers to the drumbeat of duty and desire.[30]

It has been the aim of this chapter so far to explore the socially induced individual emotional reactions to sickness and to its associates – old age and death. Revulsion, nausea, embarrassment, discomfort and disgust are hard to cope with and harder still to admit to. Yet they are not, of themselves, blameworthy. They are, at best, instructive, and for that reason it is crucial that we are aware of these individual feelings – their extent, their power and their tenacity.

When it comes to sickness, old age and death, there are surface-level value systems at work in our society. Superficially, we all agree that individuals are not to be blamed for their illnesses; that those who are old and those who are dying should be well cared for, and that economically we should invest in such care. This chapter has demonstrated, however, that beyond and underneath the surface are other very powerful, gut-level, collective psychological forces at work which may contradict – or at least challenge – our explicitly recognized and intellectually worked-out values. Programmes for social change and transformation which assume that what is going on in the head is all that matters, and that what's going on in the gut can be ignored, are problematic. For our gut-level values can be at odds with what, intellectually, we think we believe, and we can operate for years without recognizing this. Sexuality debates and discussions about racism are two spheres where this has most obviously happened. (For example, there are many who, intellectually, have no problem with gay relationships, but who feel sick at the thought of their own son having sex with another man. Likewise, there are white people who say, 'I'm not racist, but I wouldn't want my daughter to marry a black man.') I would argue that real social change can happen only when we tackle both levels, though admittedly the precise relationship between the two is hard to pin down. The least we can do is be open and honest about the horrors we feel. Crucially, we must do this not in order to close down moral debate ('Well, that's just how I feel and that's an end to it'), but to open up debates we might otherwise never have had. Our horrors tell us much about the invisible forces and power dynamics in the society we have all helped to create, and can all play a part in recreating.

'Horror' is useful shorthand for the complex cocktail of emotions so far explored, and horror speaks to us, as we have already seen, of boundary transgression. Territorial battles and the defence of boundaries are, of course, the stuff of war. It is no coincidence, then, that much modern medicine uses the language of war. Kat Duff sums this up:

> The entire discussion of health and disease in the modern world of Western medicine is couched in militaristic metaphors of attack, invasion, and defense. Disease is treated like a foreign enemy – something that must be vigilantly avoided, contained, and eradicated if necessary.

In turn, healing is not something the body does for itself, but something that must be done to it as we lie perfectly still. Our bodies are the battlegrounds in this unnamed war, and the weapons of choice in allopathic medicine – drugs and surgery – do not wave the flag of truce or fire occasional shots of warning; they drop bombs, often destroying all that surrounds as well.[31]

Susan Sontag teases out further the implications of this approach, with specific reference to cancer:

Punitive notions of disease have a long history, and such notions are particularly active with cancer. There is the 'fight' or 'crusade' against cancer; cancer is the 'killer' disease; people who have cancer are 'cancer victims'. Ostensibly, the illness is the culprit. But it is also the cancer patient who is made culpable. Widely believed psychological theories of disease assign to the luckless ill the ultimate responsibility both for falling ill and for getting well. And conventions of treating cancer as no mere disease but a demonic enemy make cancer not just a lethal disease but a shameful one.[32]

The impact of our abstract philosophical approaches to disease upon real individuals who live with illness is further explored by Duff in her account of living with Chronic Fatigue Syndrome:

I wasted a great deal of time, energy, and money, which would have been better spent learning how to live with CFIDS, rather than attempting to escape it. As the illness wore on, I struggled against the limitations it imposed, out of an old, ingrained habit of pushing limits and overcoming weariness to fulfil my ambitions and responsibilities – only to make myself sicker, over and over again. And despite my best efforts to affirm myself, and wonderfully supportive dreams and friends, I felt ashamed of myself for getting sick – and staying sick.[33]

This language of war, and the notion that each of us, as an individual, should 'fight against' and 'resist' disease when it affects us can, therefore, add guilt and shame to the symptoms of the disease itself, and can result in the increased marginalization of those already isolated by the experience of sickness. This is particularly the case where certain diseases make their way into common linguistic usage as metaphors for evil. As Sontag explains:

> Stalinism was called a cholera, a syphilis, and a cancer. To use only fatal diseases for imagery in politics gives the metaphor a much more pointed character. Now, to liken a political event or situation to an illness is to impute guilt, to prescribe punishment. This is particularly true of the use of cancer as a metaphor. It amounts to saying, first of all, that the event or situation is unqualifiedly and unredeemably wicked. It enormously ups the ante.[34]

She recognizes the problem, in our era, of finding a language adequately to express moral severity, but makes clear the impact on those with particular diseases of using those diseases as metaphors for evil: 'Trying to comprehend "radical" or "absolute" evil, we search for adequate metaphors. But the modern disease metaphors are all cheap shots. The people who have the real disease are also hardly helped by hearing the disease's name constantly being dropped as the epitome of evil.'[35]

The question arises, then – just as there are alternatives to warfare, can there not be non-violent alternative approaches to illness? Michael Wilson, as quoted earlier in this chapter, contrasts a 'healthy' society with a 'sanitized' society. A sanitized society is produced by constant purging and cleansing – by pushing undesirable elements beyond the boundaries, and policing those boundaries to prevent them from re-entering. When systematically done, this is a military operation. But Mary Douglas has pointed out that

> The quest for purity is pursued by rejection . . . It is part of

our condition that the purity for which we strive and sacrifice so much turns out to be hard and dead as a stone when we get it . . . Purity is the enemy of change, of ambiguity, of compromise . . . [yet] the yearning for rigidity is in us all. It is part of our human condition to long for hard lines and clear concepts.[36]

This, I think, is what Wilson is hinting at when he suggests that a healthy society is preferable to a sanitized one. That which is sanitized is dead.

Following Wilson's logic, then, the way to a healthy society must be through *inclusion*. If our society is to be healthy, we need to find ways of appropriately incorporating those things which we have identified as currently targets for exclusion and scapegoating – sickness (mental and physical) and death.

It is important to make clear at the outset that I am not suggesting a romanticization of sickness and death. Still less a denial of pain and suffering – or, worse, finding some overarching cosmic significance for them which renders pain not really pain, and suffering not really suffering. Both are real, and it is precisely this reality which our society encourages us, all the time, to elide. The approach I am putting forward entails speaking of sickness and death, and the pain and suffering that go with them, in a realistic and honest way. It is about acknowledging the loss involved, but also the new possibilities which are born from these experiences – without being crass by suggesting that the latter can be interpreted as providing a purpose for the former.

In the task of looking sickness squarely in the face, I rely, inevitably and appropriately, upon the words of those who have worked hard to make sense of their own illness and distress. Kat Duff, for instance, articulates the paradox of sickness when she says:

We are both diminished and enlarged through the agency of our illnesses, and so opened to the possibility of new life. The losses are many and visible; the harvested grain is smaller than the standing stalks, but so much more useful.

So Nietzsche observed, 'I doubt that such pain [the kind that compels us to descend to our ultimate depths] makes us "better"; but I know it makes us more profound . . . from such abysses, from such severe sickness, one returns newborn, having shed one's skin.'[37]

She and others help us to explore in more depth some of the characteristics of this 'harvested grain'. First, a realistic engagement with illness seems to open up the possibility of a rediscovery of human agency: 'For illness is not just something that happens to us, like a sudden sneeze or passing storm; it is part of who we are all the time. We carry within ourselves all the diseases we have had, and many we will have, as genetic inclinations, damaged organs, hidden bacteria, and sleeping cancer cells.'[38] In other words, being ill does not simply imply being 'done to', though that is often the assumption of those of us whose experience of sickness has been, mercifully, rare. Those who experience illness as contextual – a constant backdrop to their lives – rather than episodic, have access to insights about human agency and identity which others of us lack.

Second, and perhaps a related point, experience of illness forces a recognition of human limitation about which the well are prone to deliberate forgetfulness. As Audre Lorde has said, '"Living with cancer has forced me to consciously jettison the myth of omnipotence, of believing – or loosely asserting – that I can do anything." It is that myth of omnipotence, which is such a salient feature of the American spirit it has become the air we breathe without thinking, that is destroyed by the ravages of illness.'[39]

This is true as much of human psychological limitation and possibility as it is of the physical. In his book *The Noonday Demon*, Andrew Solomon movingly describes how it felt to be hit by a major depression:

In the tightest corner of my bed, split and racked by this thing no one else seemed to be able to see, I prayed to a God I had never entirely believed in, and I asked for deliverance.

I would have been happy to die the most painful death, though I was too dumbly lethargic even to conceptualise suicide. Every second of being alive hurt me. Because this thing had drained all the fluid from me, I could not even cry. My mouth was parched as well. I had thought that when you feel your worst your tears flood, but the very worst pain is the arid pain of total violation that comes after the tears are all used up, the pain that stops up every space through which you once metered the world, or the world, you. This is the presence of major depression.[40]

But, significantly, he goes on to say that, 'It is too often the quality of happiness that you feel at every moment its fragility, while depression seems when you are in it to be a state that will never pass . . . I hated being depressed, but it was also in depression that I *learned my own acreage, the full extent of my soul*'.[41] (italics mine)

Recognition of one's own limitations and new, undiscovered potential can also enhance one's understanding of and empathy with others. Jo Ind expresses this possibility in *Fat is a Spiritual Issue*:

What would I have been if I had never been a compulsive eater? The experience is now so much a part of me that any answer can only be speculative, but I do not think I would have been the kind of person I like to know. I fancied I was clever and competent. I did not succeed in everything but I succeeded in all that I cared about. I had no comprehension of why people became alcoholics, beat up their wives, stayed in bed until one o'clock or stole pocket handkerchiefs from the supermarket. I had a hard confidence that I could get out of life whatever I wanted. I imagined I was in control and that I coped.

My compulsion has given me a gentle softness. It is the softness of knowing deep down that I am who I am because of those who have loved me . . . It was their steady acceptance, their sure faith in me that freed me into an acceptance and a faith in myself. Who deserves to be loved like that? No one and everyone – humanity in general and each person in particular.[42]

To embrace the insights born of experiences of illness and sickness can result in a new vision. Suddenly the healthy and the sick are no longer two completely separate categories of people, staring at one another over an unbridgeable chasm. Rather, experiences of illness and wellness turn out to be interdependent. Kat Duff again: 'The well need to be well for the world to continue, just as the sick need to be sick so the world can be regenerated. Each has a necessary job to perform.'[43] Each are part of something larger than their own limited experience:

> The longer I am sick the more I realize that illness is to health what dreams are to waking life – the reminder of what is forgotten, the bigger picture working toward resolution. If I were to name that intelligence, that deep knowing which operates through the agency of our dreams and flesh, I would call it soul, agreeing with philosopher Morris Berman, who once said: 'Soul is another name for what the body does.'[44]

Death also needs some reinterpretation. Many people say that they want to die suddenly. After a 'good innings' they want to get up one day, go about their business as usual, then just drop dead; 'pop their clogs' (note the metaphor). No mess, no pain and no time to get maudlin about its meaning. Why is this considered the ideal? Unexpected and sudden death is certainly not ideal for those who are left behind. The shock is immense – recovery from it often unimaginable. But again, we see the influence of the capitalist context explored in Chapter 1. The ideal is to be a productive unit, self-sufficient and autonomous to the end. Only in this context is sudden death 'the best way to go'. Managing the process of palliative care for those who take a long time to die is labour-intensive and emotionally costly for all involved. But it can also be rewarding, as recent memoirs of those who have, in effect, chronicled their own deaths, have shown.[45] These writings provide an extra-ordinary view of the potential richness alongside the agony of the dying experience in the same way as those chronicling their illness and distress have challenged us to embrace the insights explored above. They challenge us to think about the process of dying – how the process of dying is as important as death itself. Miriam Taegtmeyer, a hospital doctor specializing in palliative care, offers the following reflections:

I treated a woman once who was 94. She'd been in hospital for about two weeks. First she had pneumonia, then something else went wrong, then she got a clot in her leg. The only cure was to amputate her leg, and if we didn't do that she was going to die. My boss wanted me to refer her to the surgeon to amputate the leg.

I sat down and explained all this to her. And she said, 'I want to die, of course. Now, if you don't mind I'm going home this afternoon because I haven't been home for two weeks and there's a few things I want to get organised.' So I gave her morphine for the pain from her dead leg, and we got a wheelchair organised for her, and she went home. She phoned all her friends and had them round for tea. She gave away all her prized possessions, and she told her daughter about her Will. Then she came back into hospital and an hour later she was dead.[46]

Embracing the insights of sickness and of death cause us to re-evaluate what matters. We see more clearly certain features of our social and individual value systems which may hither-to have been invisible to us. We have a greater understanding of that which we purge from our corporate life when we value an orderly 'sanitated society' above a healthy one (in Wilson's sense of the word). As Duff says, 'In our infatuation with health and wholeness, illness is one-sidedly identified with the culturally devalued qualities of quiet, introspection, weakness, withdrawal, vulnerability, dependence, self-doubt, and depression. If somebody displays any of these qualities to a great extent, he or she is likely to be considered ill and encouraged to see a doctor or a therapist.'[47] She speaks of the need constantly to revisit the insights afforded by experiences of sickness:

> Even at my sickest, when I was spending the majority of the daylight hours in bed aching, I knew that my illness was showing me facets of truth that I had missed – we had all missed, it seemed – and desperately needed. I did not want a quick cure that would tear me from those insights, though I could not admit that to most friends who wished me a speedy recovery; I wanted to find a way to carry my sickbed revelations back with me into health, to balance the lop-sided optimism, confidence, and activity of my earlier life.[48]

We are reminded, then, that the way of living that we have learned – largely influenced by the invisible value systems that are all around us – is not the only way. There are alternative definitions of usefulness, of success. There are people out there with hopes and needs and gifts and opportunities which we could never have imagined outwith the revolutionary perspective afforded by contextual (as distinct from episodic) sickness. This is not to say that we should suddenly all aspire to sickness because of the privileged access it gives us to alternative ways of looking at life. It is to say that as a society we should give more value, more opportunities to speak and be heard, to those who are too often assigned the role of (as Sontag puts it) 'life's losers'.

3

HEALING?

As it is, there are many members, yet one body. The eye cannot say to the hand, 'I have no need of you', nor again the head to the feet, 'I have no need of you.' On the contrary, the members of the body that seem to be weaker are indispensable . . . If one member suffers, all suffer together with it; if one member is honoured, all rejoice together with it.

(I Corinthians 12)

In the disintegration of physical and relational universes, how are we to be put back together?

I was once put back together in a music studio. This was both a humble and a grand setting for a story of healing. My friend, a musician, invited me into the lair of his creativity, sat me down with my tears, my fears and my regrets to listen to – to not listen to – a strong and tender beat, a massage of the soul. I found myself surrounded by fearsomely complicated technological equipment and by fearlessly elemental humanity.

The texture of his music charmed delicate emotions from obscure places. Its power erased – washed away – old patterns of interpretation, throwing the jigsaw pieces of relational life into the air. And the beat formed the boundaries beyond which I would not go – it saved me from chaos, coaxing the emergence of new patterns of thought and feeling – the creation of a new picture. This room was safety – temple of wisdom; this friend was my guide – prophet of love.

This friend was also a purveyor of stories. One day in a warm kitchen, over stew and whisky and with love, he took me on a journey into the unfamiliar – a world of spirits and divine forces which were strange to me. A world in which 'God' took on new meaning. Through his stories ranged an active God – 'up close and personal'; a mysterious and unpredictable God communicating messages that seemed bizarre except with hindsight; a God in whom was honesty, hardship, reward, deep challenge and dramatic possibility. Through his stories God changed from the cardboard cut-out god of the western Church into a divine adventurer – a multifarious, composite and demanding character.

On another occasion he said to me, 'Where I come from, the wellbeing of one is meaningless without the wellbeing of all. My success means nothing if I am the only one lifted up by it.' And I was reminded of the first confusing phrases I encountered of a certain African language. I learned the morning greeting: 'How are you?' To which the accepted and formal reply was, 'I am well if you are well.' It puzzled me that, likewise, the required response to 'Did you sleep well?' was 'I slept well if you slept well.' My western self protested: either I am well or I am not, surely? Either I slept well or badly? I realized suddenly that this is the case only if my good can be separated from your good. 'I slept well if you slept well' is not an odd reply if sleep is a communal realm of dreams and visions, in which case my sleep affects your sleep. I learned then that the most basic social greetings can relativize a lifetime's learning. And I learned through my friend that intimacy relativizes who we are.

In the disintegration of physical and relational universes, we are put back together through music, stories, food, love and friendship.

Passionate theological connections

I have so far in this book teased out our social assumptions and corporate feelings about health and wellbeing, sickness and death. I have tried to show that our experience of these concepts is embodied, not merely abstract and philosophical. I have assumed diverse experiences of embodiment from the start. I have sketched some of the features of the social backdrop against which we live out our embodied selves. In particular, it is significant that we live in an age of globalization, of money-led individualism, of swift-changing technological advance and of huge multifaceted inequality.

Some would add that we live in an age of spiritual decline. Others would concede that our era is characterized by 'secularization' but would challenge the assumption that an easy equivalence can be drawn between this and a thoroughgoing decline of spirituality. In the latter part of this chapter on healing, I will address the nature of health as a spiritual issue, looking at some of the ways in which spirituality functions in contemporary wellbeing debates. First, though, it is time to look more explicitly at some of the theological implications of the ground covered so far, and to explore some of the resulting possible directions for Christian engagement with the contemporary health and wellbeing agenda.

As a starting point, I would like to focus on one piece of theological work in particular: W. H. Vanstone's *The Stature of Waiting*.[1] Although now some twenty years old, this book introduces some fruitful and ground-breaking ideas which I find critical to our current discussion. It provides crucial theological underpinning and direction to the insights explored at the end of the chapter in this book on sickness: that is, the expressed need to find ways of incorporating the experiences of illness and death into our communal life, rather than simply rejecting them as abjection.

Vanstone's analysis of contemporary social values is that there is an overemphasis on being active, useful, independent and self-sufficient. He draws out, in particular, the implications of these values for those who are elderly and retired, and for those who are unemployed. He detects in our professed public attitudes 'a certain distaste or contempt for the status of patient, the condition of dependence'.[2] Crucial to his thought is his definition of 'patient': 'A person who becomes a patient enters into passion; he [sic] becomes one who is done to, is treated: he becomes aware of the dependence of his own destiny upon what is decided and done by others.'[3] This is accompanied, he argues, by a popular concept of God which discerns 'no dependence, no waiting, no exposure, nothing of passion or possibility, nothing of the status of patient'.[4] The upshot of this, not surprisingly, is that those who are in some way a patient are popularly considered to be ungodlike.

By way of a corrective to these popularly held values and their theological outworkings, Vanstone reassesses the passion of Jesus. He argues that it is not death itself that is central to the importance of Jesus' passion, but the fact that he was 'handed over for us' with the possibility of death. Taking issue with traditional theologies which posit a literal 'sacrificial value' in the death of Jesus, and which tend to see the passion as merely the precursor to the most important bit – his death – he argues: 'To put the matter rather crudely, it would be nearer the truth to say that the passion phase was the "greatest" phase of Jesus' life.'[5]

Furthermore, Vanstone says:

It is not 'in the nature of things' that Jesus should be exposed 'unto death' to the decisions and deeds of men: it is of His own initiative and purpose that He is handed over to be so exposed; and it is that transition itself, that willed exchange of impassibility for passion, which decisively discloses His divinity – the glory of God in him.[6]

It is so important because it reveals to us a God who waits, a God who waits because God is love.

The love theme is crucial. For it is through this that the relevance of Jesus' passion is extended to all of us.

In authentic loving there is no control of the other who is loved: that he or she will receive is beyond the power of love to ordain or know. So when our work of love is done we are destined to wait upon the outcome . . . By our activity of loving we destine ourselves, in the end, to waiting – to placing in the hands of an other the outcome of our own endeavour . . . Where love is, action is destined to pass into passion: working into waiting.[7]

It is through this theological schema that Vanstone is able to reclaim and rehabilitate the dignity of those he formerly termed patients. For now it can be seen that it is not just those who work who are potentially Godlike, but also those who wait: 'The image of God which is perceived in man's [sic] manifold capacity for activity within the world is to be perceived also in the range and variety of his capacity for passion – in the many ways and circumstances in which he waits upon the world.'[8] He makes the point that while such waiting may well be a disagreeable condition, it is not a degraded one.

I have taken time to explain Vanstone's theological thought because it is, I think, uniquely useful in opening up that realm to which Kat Duff has introduced us. As we saw in Chapter 2, she speaks of sickness as 'the reminder of what is forgotten, the bigger picture working toward resolution'.[9] And, as she rightly points out, that which has been forgotten by our society is 'the culturally devalued qualities of quiet, introspection, weakness, withdrawal, vulnerability, dependence, self-doubt'.[10] Indeed, Vanstone goes so far as to draw a complete equivalence and equality between those who work and those who wait – those who are doers and those who are patients: 'When a man [sic] receives and recognizes the beauty of a butterfly's wing he is no less enriching the totality of the world than when, by art and skill, he creates – if that were possible – a thing of equal beauty.'[11] I believe that in our contemporary social climate this theologically based, though widely ethically applicable, idea has revolutionary potential.

I would suggest, though, that Vanstone's ideas need to be taken further. What Vanstone does very effectively is to redignify those who find themselves – temporarily or permanently – in the role of patient: those who find themselves primarily *objects* of other people's activity rather than *subjects* of their own. In the process, however, there is a danger that a dualism is created and reinforced between active and passive, doer and done to. There is also a danger of glorifying the object status of people who would prefer to become subjects of their own lives – of introducing a quietist ethic when what is needed is a robust challenge to structures and systems which make people into mere objects when they needn't be so. Those who have experienced rape or sexual assault have rightly challenged theological models which glorify powerlessness or 'being done to' as a human exemplary state. While I am sure he would not intend this, there is a danger that Vanstone's thought may be used in precisely this way. Rather than merely providing the analytical and theological means by which the lower order (as popularly perceived) of the active/passive duality can be rehabilitated, I maintain that a more effective strategy is to develop an approach which aims to dissolve the duality itself. In doing this I turn to another key concept: human *agency*. I suggest that we need to learn to see and discern that which we have not been accustomed to seeing, thereby changing the terms of the debate. Let me explain.

I suggest that there is a useful parallel to be drawn here between interpretations of sickness and health and those of poverty and wealth. I have elsewhere commented on the functioning of the term 'social exclusion' in our contemporary political context.[12] It is defined as 'a shorthand label for what can happen when individuals or areas suffer from a combination of linked problems such as unemployment, poor skills, low incomes, poor housing, high crime environments, bad health and family breakdown.'[13] I have suggested that what is missing from the picture in this definition is a human agent. Social exclusion is perceived as a condition that just happens to people. The lack of agent means two things. First, it keeps our analytical eye firmly on the socially excluded and their characteristics as a body of people. It gives rise to all those value-laden questions: why can't they go to work and earn the money to lift themselves out of their excluded position? Do they have too many children? What do they spend their money on anyway? The concomitant of this, of course, is that analytical attention is simultaneously *deflected away* from the socially included. They just are. They (or should I say 'we') are simply normative and beyond criticism.

Second, this approach causes us to ignore the ways in which the excluded (or, in old-fashioned language, 'the poor') are *already* exercising human agency *now*. We fail to see, for instance, the struggle to bring up children in poverty, a willingness to undertake voluntary activity on behalf of the wider community, the necessity of negotiating a complex benefits system and developing imaginative ways of getting the best out of it, and simply surviving and remaining reasonably healthy, as being activity. We certainly don't perceive it as socially constructive living on a par with the activities of the socially included middle classes who do waged work, go on holiday and consume large amounts of goods by shopping in department stores and garden centres. The middle classes are deemed to be giving something back to society, fulfilling their side of the social contract by being active citizens, while the socially excluded are perceived as passive net recipients of society's goodies. All because we are tricked by our own concepts into ignoring certain kinds of human agency.

So to the parallel with sickness and health. If we simply adopt Vanstone's approach of reclaiming the value of passion, but leave in place the duality between active and passive, there are two dangers. First, that we will keep our analytical eye solely upon the ways in which those who are sick deal with their sickness, deflecting attention away from the ways in which the healthy negotiate their lives, and the latter's impact on the former. Second, we will ignore the complex and diverse ways in which those who are sick are already exercising their human agency, even in the midst, perhaps, of apparent passivity. In other words, in rethinking all of this, it is not enough simply to say that those who are inactive are also, in a Christian framework, accorded human dignity in the scheme of things. Although that is, of course, the case. It is also important to recognize that our normative ideas about what counts as being 'subject' and what counts as being 'object' have tricked us into seeing a duality where really there is a spectrum and a continuum. For each of us is a complex mix of both subject and object, and how we negotiate the balance between the two is a matter of human agency. The point is that we are all, each and every one of us, on a health/sickness, ability/disability continuum. Our place on the continuum constantly changes; what matters is how we exercise our agency *wherever we are on it*. What we often need help with are the times of transition and change – the times when the old ways of exercising our human agency no longer fit our new embodied reality, but we have yet to learn new ways of being human.

Here's an example that might help to make clearer what I am getting at. If a colleague phones in to work and says, 'I'm staying in bed today, I'm not well', the chances are that we will assume that this person has 'given in' to a bug and – for a while at least – is destined to languish powerlessly in bed at home as 'object' of said bug. Our socially induced values will enable us to offer sympathy to such a person for approximately a week. A bit longer if they are lucky. But on closer examination, we see that the subject/object split in this case is not as simple as first appears. In such a situation some of us will lie completely comatose in bed, some will drag themselves to the sofa and watch daytime TV, some will drift in and out of sleep and read a novel in the meantime, and others will sneak the laptop under the covers and send emails in defiance of the illness. Each of these options involves an element of both subject and object status. If we pay our aforementioned colleague a supportive visit – perhaps to take them some shopping – we will no doubt make a subconscious assessment of how ill they seem to be to us, and wonder whether we would have 'given in' more easily or less easily. Indeed, the point at which each of us bows to the inevitable in the face of the onset of illness varies enormously. We each have our own way of dealing with it: our own way of exercising our agency.

And what if I phone in to work and announce that I'm staying at home not because I'm ill, but because I feel a bit under the weather and if I don't take a day off I know (because I listen to my body) that I will *become* ill? Arguably, most employers would frown upon such behaviour, but it could be said that this is a most responsible approach. Such a decision involves exercising agency just as much, though in a different way, as in the more common strategy of soldiering on until we are left incapacitated for a fortnight, and have infected large numbers of our colleagues in the process. The latter is, unfortunately, the normative and socially sanctioned approach to illness in our society. The point is that human agency can be exercised through apparently passive behaviour as well as through apparent activity – and in some cases, most effectively so.

To recap, we have endorsed Vanstone's theological rationale for valuing times of 'passion' alongside times of activity. But we have also supplemented his thinking by looking at ways to dissolve the duality between active and passive, doer and done to, replacing it with a continuum, and by focusing on the complexity of human agency. I believe that our discussion so far gives rise to two new theological directions which require further examination. Vanstone's thinking links with another point explored by Kat Duff: 'The well need to be well for the world to continue, just as the sick need to be sick so the world can be regenerated. Each has a necessary job to perform.'[14] The nature of *human interdependence* is therefore a key theological theme, and we will return to this soon. But first I want to explore another theological theme by revisiting the parallel between sickness/health and poverty/wealth.

In our discussion about the definition of social exclusion I suggested that rather than allow an elision of human agency through an assumption that exclusion just happens, we need to focus upon the processes by which the included are included in order to understand how the excluded become excluded. As a matter of theological and ethical imperative, we need now to make a similar move regarding health and sickness. Though particular diseases may strike us by chance, in general sickness and health do not just happen to people any more than social exclusion just happens. They are, in large part, the outcome of particular life experiences, affected by particular personal circumstances, influenced by structural social, economic and attitudinal forces. Rethinking death, disability and ill-health, as I have suggested in this book that we need to do, must go hand in hand with building our passion for protest against the structural injustice that underlies it. As theologians and church people we need to be asking: why are some people consistently less healthy than others – for instance, those who are economically poor, members of ethnic minority groups, those who are survivors of abuse and violence? Eric Petrie throws down the gauntlet in his book *Unleashing the Lion* when he says: 'The Church has forgotten to engage in the struggle with the injustice of sickness . . . the Christian community claims to be biased towards the marginalized but leaves the struggle with the injustice of illness to medical practitioners who mistakenly see the battle as one against death not injustice.'[15]

I repeat: health and sickness do not just happen. In our society they are enjoyed and endured disproportionately, depending upon which social groupings we belong to. We cannot take an embodied approach to health and wellbeing without noticing that some bodies are more equal than others. It is worth taking a bit of time now to focus on the health inequalities that abound in our social context, thereby revealing how the majority of us exercise our agency most of the time to tolerate such injustices (most of us are in the majority sometimes even if we are not in the majority all the time).

Let's start with the basics: food. Without good food, good health is impossible. Yet we live in a society where large numbers of people have no affordable access to the kinds of foodstuffs that contribute to a healthy diet. In-depth research into this phenomenon has been carried out very recently in Sandwell, West Midlands – an area of very high economic deprivation. The resulting report highlights how structural economic issues impact upon what are widely assumed to be issues of individual choice. It says this:

> The appearance of food deserts is a consequence of the free market approach to food retailing, and inequalities, over the last few decades . . . If the maps generated in this research were of streets with or without running water, or with or without substandard housing, they would rightly warrant urgent remedial action. Hitherto, food has been regarded as a domestic issue, where people are free to make their own, private choices about how they spend their

money.' [The conclusion of the researchers underlines the importance of what might otherwise be considered a marginal issue] '. . . food, like water and shelter, is a fundamental human right. If we value life, we need only make sure people have access to healthy food. This research has demonstrated that many people in Sandwell do not enjoy reasonable access to healthy food.'[16]

The appearance of food deserts in our relatively affluent society will not be news to those working with anti-poverty lobby groups, who have long worked to highlight the health impact of economic inequality. The Child Poverty Action Group, for instance, reminds us consistently that poverty and social exclusion are associated with poor health. To give one example:

> A survey of English adults in 1998 asked people whether their health was good or 'less than good'. Those most likely to report 'less than good' were from manual social classes; on incomes below £10,000; economically inactive; with no qualifications; in local authority housing; and single unemployed people. The General Household Survey has also revealed that people from manual groups have been more likely to report longstanding illness and suffer from conditions like musculo-skeletal problems and heart complaints.[17]

Many of those living in relative poverty in Britain report sickness or disability, most commonly asthma, bronchitis and eczema. Ill-health is associated with the stress of poverty, inability to meet extra expenses caused by illness, and not being able to heat homes sufficiently. CPAG tells us that the widening income inequalities of the 1980s and early 1990s have been accompanied by a parallel trend in health inequalities, although the precise causal relationship is still debated. These inequalities are also, apparently, reflected in death rates: 'Although overall death rates for babies and young children have declined over time, disparities remain . . . The poorest areas have failed to match the overall improvement; in London's Bethnal Green, child mortality rates for males were higher in 1992 than in 1950.'[18] In a discussion document on the health of men produced by Worcestershire Health Authority it is documented:

> There is a four-fold difference in mortality from accidents and suicide between the most affluent and the least affluent men in this country. For lung cancer, this variation is even greater – there is a five-fold difference. Social class V males experience a three times greater death rate from stroke and heart disease then men in social class I.[19]

In Chapter 1 of this book I identified good relationships and self-esteem as being of crucial importance to human health and wellbeing. Yet we live in a social context where sexual and physical violation are common. Some estimate that as many as one in four women – and a significant minority of men – has some experience of sexual abuse, with many abused as children. Domestic violence is also common. As defined by the Flare West Mercia Domestic Violence Helplines Project: 'Domestic Violence is the physical, emotional or sexual abuse of women and children by someone close to them, usually a partner or ex-partner.' The documentation associated with this project goes on to state:

> 1 in every 4 women will experience Domestic Violence at some time during their lifetime . . . Every three days in Britain a woman is murdered by a partner or ex-partner. Approximately 20,000 women and 30,000 children in Britain stay in refuges or safe houses every year, leaving family, friends, jobs, schools, pets, homes and personal possessions behind them. The loss felt is the same as a major bereavement, along with fear, isolation, confusion and loneliness. Approximately 70% of children who stay in refuges have also been abused by their father. Over 25,000 women called Women's Aid National Domestic Violence helpline during 2000.

In terms of erosion of trust, obliteration of self-worth and the resulting damage to a person's capacity to build sustaining and creative relationships with others, such abuse and violence can be seen only as tragically implicated in the undermining of public health in this country.

Sometimes (though I stress only sometimes), those who are developing strategies to survive abuse and violence develop forms of behaviour which can be disruptive and damaging to themselves and to others. Sometimes such people end up in prison, where another whole set of structural health inequalities kick in. Briefly, as one policy discussion paper recently put it:

> Prisons isolate inmates from their families and social networks. Suicide and self-harm are not uncommon among prisoners. Opportunities to choose friends are limited and unconventional sexual practices can lead to emotional problems, sexually transmitted diseases and violence. Boredom is common, introspection results, hypochondriasis is rife. Drug abuse is promoted (by other inmates), dependence is common, debt ensues and violence is frequently the result. Prison culture frowns upon the weak or emotional and may prevent those in need from seeking help. Amongst those serving longer sentences the prison regime rapidly promotes institutionalisation and dependence.[20]

Another key issue which I identified in Chapter 1 as important to health and wellbeing was that of identity. Our bodies are 'raced' and 'gendered', and our sexuality is crucial to our self-understanding. But these markers of identity also place us within social power structures with implications for health. Young gay men, for instance, are much more likely to commit suicide than their heterosexual counterparts; lesbians are more likely to abuse alcohol than straight women. Both these factors stem from the stress of institutionalized discrimination at work, school, home and society in general against gay men, lesbians and bisexual people.

Women and men have different health needs, and use health services differently. As the aforementioned report on the health of men in Worcestershire points out: 'A traditional view of men as providers and protectors who are strong in mind and body has compounded the difficulties experienced by males in the face of rapid shifts in the structure and process of our society.'[21] The report goes on to suggest:

> While men in general suffer more disease they are not permitted to be more expressive about it. They conform to a socially prescribed male role where attitudes to illness are robust and mechanical metaphors are used to describe the body's workings . . . These attitudes and behaviours are reflected in the way that men use health services, which is characterised by less frequent and much later consultation than by women.[22]

The flip side of this gendering of health is that social constructions of femininity land women with the responsibility of being gatekeepers for health on behalf of male partners and children. The responsibility for buying and preparing food and maintaining comfortable and hygienic living conditions still falls disproportionately on women – as does the maintenance of family relationships. When illness and/or disability occur, it is usually women who are the mediators between their families and health and social services. Most of the unpaid caring responsibilities in our society are borne by women.

Racial identity is also important in terms of health differentials, though the issues are complex. As King's Fund research has recently pointed out, 'systematic inequalities continue to exist for black and minority ethnic groups in terms of their experiences of both health and health care'.[23] It sums up the issues as follows:

> Generally, belonging to a certain ethnic group per se does not directly lead to better or worse health. There are a few diseases or conditions, such as the haemoglobinopathies

(thalassaemia and sickle cell disease for example) that are strongly associated with particular ethnic groups because of their genetic basis. However, research increasingly shows that a considerable proportion of ill health in black and minority ethnic groups is more closely linked to their socio-economic status, environmental and employment conditions. It has been argued that over-representation of black and minority ethnic groups in lower socio-economic classes, poor housing and unemployment reflects wider societal racism.[24]

When it comes to mental health specifically, however, there are some very stark and well-documented differentials. These were rather devastatingly summed up in a parliamentary debate in November 2001 about David Bennett, aka 'Rocky', a black patient in a psychiatric ward, who died on 31 October 1998 after being restrained by at least three, possibly five, staff for 25 minutes.

In that debate Helen Clark (Peterborough) said:

In February, the report of the ethnic issues project group in the Royal College of Psychiatrists, which it kindly sent to me, stated: 'African-Caribbean individuals are over-represented among admissions to psychiatric hospitals, especially as compulsorily detained patients. Various reports have shown that [such patients] on the whole receive a more coercive spectrum of care. Among offender patients, African-Caribbean men were 26 times more likely than white men to be detained on criminal sections.' It also cites research that suggests that psychiatrists tend to over-predict dangerousness in black people, and that such bias leads to a more restrictive outcome.

I understand that evidence of racial inequality in mental health services has been available for 20 or even 30 years. All this shows that black people are more likely than whites to be removed by the police to a place of safety under section 136 of the Mental Health Act 1983, retained in hospital under sections 2, 3 and 4 of the Act, diagnosed as suffering from schizophrenia or another form of psychotic illness, detained in locked wards of psychiatric hospitals, and given higher doses of medication. The research also shows that black people are less likely than white people to receive appropriate and acceptable diagnosis of, or treatment for, possible mental illness at an early stage, and to receive treatments such as psychotherapy and counselling.[25]

It is clear, therefore, that we experience health and wellbeing, ill-health and sickness, through the diversity of our embodiment. None of us is a 'generic person'. Each of us has a particular identity. Race, gender, class and sexuality are all important, as are a whole host of other factors. These factors combine to affect our notions of what constitutes health; our expectations regarding the kind of health we can expect for ourselves and others; our access to a range of health services, and the way in which we negotiate that access. It ought to be axiomatic, but it is nonetheless worth saying, that any Christian theological engagement with issues of health and wellbeing must *work with* the richness and diversity that constitutes our human communities, but *work against* the inequalities and structural injustices outlined above. It must challenge an economic system which encourages huge differentials between the wealthiest and the poorest, and it must challenge systems which continue to institutionalize racism, male domination and heterosexism.

Now to the second theological theme which I identified through my discussion of Vanstone: human interdependence. For it is only in a world where interdependence is assumed that those who wait can be equally as valuable as those who work. It could be argued that we have a well-established system in this country for expressing this vision: it's called the National Health Service. But what is its future, and why should we care?

'Just as Well' was a day conference held in May 2000 organized jointly by Worcestershire Health Authority and the Church of England Board for Social Responsibility in the

Diocese of Worcester. The conference had two aims: first, to
address inequalities in health; and second, to explore the role
of religious and faith communities in the contemporary health
agenda. One of the keynote speakers, Ian Wylie (then Head of
Corporate Affairs at the Kind's Fund), addressed the issue of
'Health for all; or just for me? Promoting health as a social
responsibility'. It is worth quoting this unpublished paper at
length because in it he expresses in very clear terms what is at
stake, politically – and by extension theologically – in current
debates about the nature and future of the NHS.

He began by revisiting the foundations of the NHS in 1946.
At that time, as Wylie put it,

> People were comfortable about pooling resources. They
> were also comfortable with the notion of contributing
> unequally. Hadn't our fittest, youngest, brightest con-
> tributed most to the war but had been willing to benefit
> equally from the outcome? The NHS was created from that
> thinking. It was a redistributive system.

The Government has recently put a great deal more money
into the Health Service than it has ever received before. But
with the money comes the challenge to modernize. But what
does modernization mean? Wylie pointed out that it can mean
one of two things: that the NHS provides the highest quality,
most responsive and most accessible health services to maximize the health of the population; or the NHS provides *me*
with the services that *I* want, in a way that is acceptable and
convenient *to me and my family*, to maximize *my* health. Ian
Wylie's conclusion was that 'For this Government modernization seems to mean both. The trouble is, you can't have both.
They are two different ways of looking at the world.' The first
is a model based on recognition of human interdependence,
the second is one based on individualistic consumerism.

He then illustrated this with a concrete example:

> Say next winter I get flu. I need to go to work so I go to my
> GP and ask for relenza. The GP says she isn't going to

provide me with relenza because her Primary Care Trust has prioritized heart disease treatment. I don't have heart disease, I have flu. I want relenza, and I'm not going to get what I want. Is that fair? Well, yes, actually it is, according to health for all, if someone is in greater need . . . If we want health care for me and for now, then we will have to give up on the NHS, because that is not what the NHS was designed to do.

He reinforced this with another example:

In fact, we don't need to think to next winter. Look at last winter and the so-called 'winter crisis'. During that time, particularly just after New Year, a lot of routine operations were cancelled in hospitals up and down the country as the NHS switched its resources to deal with a number of sick, frail, often elderly, people who needed hospital care. So? Big deal. That's what a managed, shared resource does. It prioritizes need and from the resources available, offers support based on measures of risk.

I suggest that Wylie's vision of the NHS as a practical structure making manifest the ideal of 'health for all' is precisely the kind of vision which deserves Christian theological endorsement. Being clear about the difference between 'health for all' and 'health for me' is not easy in our political context. Against a rights-based, individualistic, market-led philosophical backdrop it might seem vaguely ludicrous to acquiesce in finding oneself on a waiting list for non-urgent treatment. But if the NHS is managed according to the philosophy of health for all, that's exactly what we might expect to happen. And if we believe in the Christian vision of human interdependence, then that's what we should be championing. Where we are bound to protest, however, is when we detect that decisions about who has to wait the longest are based on considerations other than the prioritization of need: if, for instance, it were to become clear that those who are less likely to complain were being put to the bottom of the list so that those who are more vocal and articulate might be kept happy. A Christian theological approach that works against unequal treatment must be alert to how decisions about priorities are made, assessing the visions of fairness that lie behind such methodologies.

Health-promoting communities?

I have so far looked at two themes of theological significance arising from our exploration and critique of Vanstone: human interdependence, and the ways in which structural social inequalities are implicated in experiences of health and sickness in our society. But there are other important and related issues which arise when we consider Christian theological engagement with contemporary health and wellbeing agendas. Here we will now explore three: diversity, love and community.

Bishop Peter Selby has made the following comment:

The question is, what do we value in the world of health? The trend seems to be towards human uniformity and homogeneity. But is not the body politic, the body social, better for having access to experiences of difference? Do they not offer something which is a component of the health of us all? What would the 'cure' of all mental illness have done to the store of human endeavour throughout the ages? In particular, where would poetry, art and theology be without it?[26]

Jo Ind touches on similar ground in expressing the liberatory vision of Jesus which was important to her in the context of her eating disorder. She says this:

The Jesus I believed in was one I saw in a performance of *Godspell*. He rescued those paralysed in sameness by making them more themselves. He gave the punk rocker another safety pin, he untangled the belly dancer's grass skirt and he restored the red nose to the clown. This was

Jesus – not a Jesus who turned them into Super Christians but one who set them free to be who they really were. And the more themselves they became, the more different from each other they became. The big, gutsy woman became more raunchy, the humorous fool became more amusing, the elegant man became more sophisticated.[27]

The Christian tradition is about the promotion of human flourishing, of 'life in all its fullness'. We might therefore assume that it goes without saying that Christian communities should be health-promoting communities. But Selby raises for us the question: what on earth does that *mean*? We have already discovered that there is no such thing as a generic person, so it is safe to assume that there is no such thing as a generic healthy person or a generic sick person. We have also discovered that there is a huge diversity of possible ways in which we each express our agency as we move around on the health/sickness continuum. So neither can there be a single generic blueprint according to which a transformation from 'sick' to 'well' might be made. Indeed, if Selby is right, there is even doubt about whether it is always appropriate to expect transformation in that particular direction. Where, then, does all this complexity leave us theologically?

At this point I would like to return to my reflections on the story of Sarah in the first chapter of this book. I concluded that those who named her 'obese, unkempt Caucasian' were guilty of an unjust misnaming of the worst kind. I believe that appropriate naming is the key to a justice-promoting theological engagement with questions of health and wellbeing. I will now explain what I mean, drawing upon several examples, and making links with Vanstone's theological foundations with which I began this section.

A recent article in the *Guardian* recounted the life story of Ron Coleman. Once a 'chronic schizophrenic' he was, in his own words, 'as mad as they come'. As the article puts it, 'When not compulsorily detained in hospital, commuters might have spotted him at Manchester's Piccadilly station, bearded and dishevelled, shouting back at abusive voices that tormented him.' Apparently doctors tried to 'cure' Ron for 12 years. He was given cocktails of anti-psychotic medication and 40 courses of electro-convulsive therapy: 'It all failed. He had as good as resigned himself to his psychiatrists' view that his voices were an "auditory hallucination" – a symptom of schizophrenia. His voices were not real, he was told. He should ignore them.' In 1991, however, his support worker suggested that he attend a meeting of the Manchester-based group Hearing Voices Network, a self-help organization for people, many of them diagnosed schizophrenic, who hear voices. The article continues:

> Coleman recalls: 'In the meeting someone said to me: "Ron, your voices are real." Now imagine what it is like to think the world was flat and to discover it was round. I carried the words "your voices are real" around with me for years. I was, in a sense, blinded by truth. Like Paul on the road to Damascus.'

Apparently Coleman's subsequent recovery was rapid:

> With help from the network, which he co-ordinated from 1992 to 1995, he began to work with, rather than against, his voices. He assessed what and who they represented and was given the support to relate them to his childhood sexual experiences – and to see how it was the denigrating voice of his abuser that lay at the heart of his distress.[28]

There are many ways in which those who are more powerful impose their interpretation of what is the case on those who are less powerful. In the context of health, the patient (according to Vanstone's definition of the terms as well the narrower common-sense meaning) is expected to take as fact the interpretations of medical professionals as to their symptoms, prognosis and the most appropriate forms of treatment. But Sarah's story showed us that what is presented as fact by professionals, or common sense by society at large, is not necessarily straightforwardly so.

Let's recall how politics surrounding the HIV virus developed. Remember how swiftly common-sense social values ascribed the designation 'AIDS victim' to those who became HIV-positive? As knowledge accumulated, however, it became clear that whether and when those who were HIV-positive would develop AIDS-related conditions was by no means predictable. It also became clear that when those who were HIV-positive got together to support one another and to share their experiences of living with the virus, they began to develop completely different interpretations of the meaning of their lives vis-à-vis HIV. The most striking motif in this regard was the way in which 'AIDS victims' became 'PWAs' (people living with AIDS) and 'people living with HIV'. In short, they refused an ontology completely determined by the presence of one particular virus in their blood, and they resisted social values which presented as fact a status which they considered demeaning. In the terminology used earlier in this chapter, they exercised their agency and in so doing made the journey from object status to subject status.

There are, of course, other examples of such resistance. Many people with cancer refuse to regard themselves as 'cancer victims', locked in a battle with an enemy disease, though the popular media still talks predominantly in these terms. Many talk of 'embracing' cancer, or 'living with' it – and this happens in the case of other diseases too.

Given all that has been said so far about the theological value of recognizing the diversity of human expressions of agency, I believe that an important role for the Christian community is to support people in naming their own experiences of wellness and illness. In the process the Christian community will be joining with a whole host of advocacy and self-help groups, and with a growing number of health professionals who have themselves been influenced by movements which, in health care language, 'empower service-users'. Academics in the field of health and social care have documented these philosophical changes. In an article focusing on holistic approaches to mental distress, Jerry Tew sums up very neatly what is at stake:

What should lie at the heart of a holistic value base must be a commitment to engage honestly with all the fractured and contradictory elements that may constitute a person's experience and social relationships . . . Such an approach would require a commitment to hear and take seriously what people may have to say about their mental distress: the content of their experiences, and the meanings, histories and aspirations that *they* attach to them . . . This quality of listening to people *on their terms* is something that users have consistently identified as lacking within much of existing service provision, and explicitly challenges those traditions of mental health practice which have sought to classify, diagnose or interpret such experiences *for* people.[29] (italics his)

Towards the beginning of this chapter, I touched upon Vanstone's suggestion that love is what links Jesus' experience of passion with ours:

In loving one offers no limited proportion of what one has and is: one expends, or at least makes available, the whole of one's resources. But this unlimited expenditure is made for the sake of an other – in order that an other may receive; and, whenever that other is no mere extension of oneself but truly an other, then it must remain in doubt whether that other will in fact receive.[30]

Vanstone's approach helps us to see that an authentic love ethic, whether expressed in religious or secular terms, involves allowing another to be precisely that: an other. It means allowing people to name themselves and interpret their own experience. It means not using the power that we may have to name others' experience *for them* because we think we know best. This is hard. This is waiting. There is a challenge here for the Christian community, just as there is a challenge for the community of mental health professionals in Ron Coleman's experience and his interpretation of it. For it is arguable that the Christian community is no more an embodiment of Vanstone's vision of love at this point in time than any other institution in this country which aims to promote human wellbeing.

Like any other institution, the Christian community lives according to more or less rigid structures of received wisdom. These are not easy to pin down because they operate, for the most part, very subtly and invisibly. In the context of health and wellbeing, one positive element to Christian received wisdom is that it is axiomatic that those who are ill should be cared for by the community and included in it. On the other hand, however, it is clear that power lies with the healthy and the well, and that those who are sick are positioned, in structural terms, in a relatively powerless position. This is so in practical terms (i.e., in terms of who's in charge and who does what), but also in philosophical terms (whose interpretation of the world and its meaning are taken as normative). This is highlighted very powerfully by Jo and John Austen in an article on disability and discipleship. It is written in partnership: Jo contributes from her perspective as a Christian with severe cerebral palsy; John from his perspective as an Anglican priest.

> Going about and doing good is difficult if you can't go about. Matthew 25 is a powerful call to active discipleship . . . It is a passage beloved of those who are activists . . . For Jo, however, the reverse is true. She resents the presupposition that to be a disciple of Christ means going and doing things. Severe disability has meant huge limitations on what she can do, so this passage is something of a turn-off or indeed a source of guilt . . . The passage, despite having inspired many people down the centuries, can lead preachers both to categorise some disabled people as the recipients of other Christians' discipleship and also to emphasise their inability to join in.[31]

The test of this power dynamic is to what extent the normatively 'well' community is willing to be changed by the experience of those who are ill, or of those who have disabilities. The lived experience of those who have passed from one category to the other is that the Christian community's ability to be so changed is strictly limited. Models of professional ministry, for instance, assume a level of activity and mobility which only the normatively well and able-bodied can attain. Those who have been normatively well but have become ill or developed disabilities have found that the institution finds it impossible to work with their new limitations, but also – perhaps more significantly – to accommodate the new insights and gifts to which they feel their new experience gives them access. They find themselves on the margins where once they were at the centre.

Earlier I suggested that our analytical focus tends to rest upon how those who are sick deal with their experience, thereby making invisible the ways in which those who are healthy go about being healthy. Yet it is the latter which provides the overarching framework for the former. There's nothing new in this, for those with more power always get to set the terms of the debate, just as it is always those with less power who are required to do the analytical legwork. When that analytical work has been done, it is usually found to be of immense value to those who share the world of the less powerful, but the insights are rarely embraced by the powerful. Precisely because they are powerful, they don't think they need them. In *The Alchemy of Illness*, Kat Duff expresses her perception as an ill person about the world of the well: 'Frankly, from the viewpoint of illness, healthy people seem ridiculous, even a touch dangerous, in their blinded busyness, marching like soldiers to the drumbeat of duty and desire . . . Their world, to which we once belonged and will again most likely, seems unreal, like some kind of board game that could fold up at any minute.'[32] I suggest that it is in the interests of those who are well to choose to learn from such insights now, rather than wait until they have no choice.

It is in a community context that such learning can happen, which is why Christian and other religious communities can be so valuable. But I believe that the Christian community needs to ask itself some serious questions about what it means to be 'a community'. Maggie is a woman with depression who was interviewed by Andrew Solomon in his book *The Noonday Demon: An Anatomy of Depression*. She expressed her need for Christian community in the following way:

> The Church is an exoskeleton for those whose endoskeleton has been eaten away by mental illness. You pour yourself into it and adapt to its shape. You grow a spine within it. Individualism, this breaking of ourselves away from everything else, has denigrated modern life. The Church says we should act first within our communities, and then as members of the body of Christ, and then as members of the human race. It's so non-twenty-first-century American, but it's so important. I take from Einstein the idea that humans are labouring under an 'optical delusion' that each of them is separate from the others, and from the rest of the material world, and from the universe – when in fact we are all entirely interconnected parts of the universe. For me, Christianity is the study of what real love, useful love, consists of – and of what constitutes attention.[33]

In line with Maggie's experience, the value of the community aspects of faith traditions – particularly to mental health – is being recognized with increasing frequency within the secular world of health and social care. A recent article in the *Health Service Journal*, for instance, stated:

> Being part of a faith community enables regular close contact with valued others, and the experience of being valued helps build self-esteem and healthy coping strategies. It has been shown to reduce significantly the risk of suicide in young people and the likelihood of depression and anxiety, particularly among women. And adherence to a particular faith tradition realigns an individual's thinking and can enable them to cope constructively with trauma and illness, though the implications of this for health depend on how the religious coping manifests itself.[34]

It may be that religious communities are some of the few
places in our fragmented society where people can experience
the sense of being part of something bigger and mattering to
someone beyond themselves. When religious communities
are appropriately inclusive, they can provide a felt experience
of interdependence. But such inclusion does not just happen.
It has to be worked for. In terms of mental health, Lynne
Friedli makes the following comment about the potential of
faith communities:

> Recognition of how common mental health problems are
> and the extent of the shared experience of mental distress
> within a congregation can provide a strong foundation
> from which to explore the meaning and value of mental
> health promotion within the expression of religious faith.
> From this perspective, faith communities have an important
> role in increasing understanding of mental health issues
> and challenging stigma and discrimination.[35]

There is clearly an agenda here for clergy and lay education
and development across Christian denominations. Opportunities for training in the nature of mental health and mental
health promotion are most important and constructive. In my
own diocese various initiatives have been piloted, particularly
training for clergy, offered ecumenically and organized in
partnership with the Health Authority. The aim is to optimize
the potential of church congregations to be communities promoting mental health.

Developments and requirements in the secular world can
often provide the motivating force which causes congregations to work systematically to educate themselves about
issues of importance. This has certainly been the case on
issues of child protection. The Disability Discrimination Act
(DDA) has precipitated much constructive questioning and
exploration of late about the nature of inclusive churches. In
preparing a collection of stories for a briefing sheet on the
DDA for the Diocese of Worcester, I talked to several church
members about the ways in which they had felt included and

excluded within their congregations. One woman told the story of her son Pete, now 35, who has severe learning disabilities.

> Church has been central to Pete. My husband and I have always believed that Pete should come along with us, and be with us whenever we were going to worship. That was a bit hard in one place, the first place we worshipped, because I was asked could I not bring the baby who might cry, the handicapped baby, into the pram service, it would be upsetting to the other mothers. That was quite a regular story, though we moved on from that church to another where, no matter what the difficulties, Peter – as part of our family and in his own right – was accepted. Within the church, Peter has a unique ministry. Yet he is someone who, even today, some would call a 'right-off', 'a vegetable', and who is economically 'unviable'. In today's climate we think only of profit and forget the individual worth of a person. It's the attitude of church members towards those who are 'different' that matters most. There's no two ways about it, Pete is different. But also in our little church there is someone who obviously drinks; someone with a mental illness who has a wife with moderate learning difficulties. There are several very old people. We often joke and call our church 'the special needs church', and there is a real care for one another there. It's how we cope with all our differences that matters.

As has already been explored in this book, there are many subconscious fears and repulsions at work in any group of people. Christian communities are no different. There are many stories of incredible accommodation of those who are 'different' within the Christian community. But there are also many stories of inclusion that is paternalistic and patronizing, that does not allow people to name themselves and to be themselves. Take the approach to lesbians and gay men, for instance. Official church documents still insist on naming as 'homosexual' or 'homophile' those whose sexual orientation is towards those of the same gender. This is in spite of the fact that for many years members of that community have insisted that they prefer to be named lesbian or gay. Inclusion that does not allow people to say 'This is who I am' is not inclusion at all. We may be born, in our society, with a natural instinct to welcome difference – but if we are, it is soon expunged from us. We need to educate ourselves about difference – equip ourselves with the tools to ask appropriate and constructive questions of ourselves and others so that our experience of community and of interdependence is enhanced.

My observation is that the Christian community has at its heart instances both of great failure and of great possibility. Years of facilitating discussions about sexuality within churches convinced me that their members are often strangers to one another. If Christian communities are to promote health and wellbeing within themselves and more widely in society as a whole, Christians need to talk to one another more. We need to talk to one another about things that matter, about things that are deep and significant: personal relationships, sexuality, faith and meaning. It is a matter of some irony that many members of Christian communities are too embarrassed to talk to one another about the precise thing that draws them to church in the first place: their faith journey. Many are ashamed of their doubts, and fear being revealed as fraudulent – as not 'proper' Christians. Others assume that they are theologically ignorant and have nothing to offer anyone else. But it is only in finding and developing the language to do this talking that insight will be gained: about individuals – their diversity and interdependence – and about the structures of power which operate between individuals and within Christian institutional life.

Searching for the spiritual

The sacred . . . has left us without leaving us alone.[36]

'To be with other people', 'to connect with our history', 'as a mark of respect': these were the reasons given by some of the thousands who queued for hours to file past the coffin of Queen Elizabeth the Queen Mother as she lay in state in Westminster Hall, London, in April 2002. The most common comment from journalists covering the story, however, was how inarticulate the people were. They reported that nobody was *really* able to express why they were doing what they were doing. The predominant feeling seemed to be an inchoate sense of imperative: 'I don't know why, but I just felt I had to be here.'

Apparently within hours of the tragic train crash at Ladbroke Grove in October 1999, passers-by had begun to place flowers on the road bridge which passed over the railway line nearest to the crash. As time went by, bouquets accumulated, including some from relatives and friends of those who had died. Sometimes, families of those killed on our roads turn the fatality sites into roadside shrines, tying flowers and soft toys to lamp-posts and road signs. When there are major disasters, such activity causes much angst to those in Local Authority emergency planning departments who are charged with deciding what to do with the mementos (if that is what they are); how to dispose of them in an appropriate manner. To know that, you've got to understand what's at stake – what is their significance. And no one is really quite sure. On anniversaries of such tragedies, symbols appear again. Remember how we were encouraged on the anniversary of the Dunblane shootings to light a candle and place it in our window?

If the sacred really has left us, how do we explain these phenomena? Why this imperative to mark symbolically the site of tragedy? If we really are a secular society, why the demand for services of remembrance and memorial? The sacred echoes noisily – a force in the present expressed, for the most part, in the language of the past. It is an influence struggling to be rearticulated, but without having yet found a new mother tongue. This is a life force at odds with the normative philosophical framework of post-Enlightenment rationalism, devoid as it is of divine imagination. Sometimes we feel the loss, though usually we miss hardly anything at all.

In extremis, it seems that even the most secular liberal among us – even those whose religious imaginations have been flattened, emptied out, disqualified by social context; even those whose minds and intellects find no room for divine intervention – somehow can imagine another's care and attention making a difference; making an impact in ways beyond our understanding. In extremis, most of us make room for the invisible, the mysterious, the incomprehensible. To return to a quote from Andrew Solomon, 'In the tightest corner of my bed, split and racked by this thing no one else seemed to be able to see, I prayed to a God I had never entirely believed in, and I asked for deliverance.'[37]

Some have argued that we have, as human beings, a kind of God-shaped gap or essential spiritual core, transcending time and place, manifesting itself differently according to circumstance. I don't know about that. But I would argue that in extreme circumstances, when meaninglessness and futility threaten to overwhelm order and rationality, human beings need forms of linguistic and symbolic expression which speak of mystery, meaning and transcendence in ways which connect with, but go beyond, everyday speech. Health and sickness, birth and death, are, of course, life experiences which call forth both the need and the possibility of such forms of expression.

The severe and definite limitations of scientific medical language are summed up by Gillian Rose, expressing how she felt when her oncologist suggested that further treatment for her cancer would not be beneficial:

This sentencing . . . accelerated my release and departure from the disintegrating authority of conventional medicine. Medicine and I have dismissed each other. We do not have enough command of each other's language for the exchange to be fruitful. It is as if, exiled for ever into a foreign tongue, you learn the language by picking up words and phrases, even sentences, but never proceed to grasp the underlying principles of grammar and syntax, which would give you the freedom to use the language creatively and critically . . .

If I am mute, then so is medicine. It can no more fathom my holistic and spiritual matrix than I can master its material syntax.[38]

The language of meaning on which we rely, in which we – as a secular society – encourage one another to place our trust can, in the face of illness, death and other crises, seem suddenly and irrevocably worthless. There are certain life experiences which can render everything we have valued – health, self-sufficiency, wealth, independence – suddenly meaningless. At this point we begin (or resume with new vigour) the search for an alternative language of meaning. Organized religion has traditionally offered such a language, but the question for our contemporary culture is: does it and can it still? If so, how?

When he wrote *Health is for People* in 1976, Michael Wilson was clearly also perplexed by such questions. In the book he suggests that the fading out of religious language is made more complex by the fact that 'health' itself has, in some ways, replaced 'God' as our highest human aspiration. In the following passage, which is worth quoting at length, he sums up many of the themes so far explored in this book. He draws our attention to the question of how quality of life, rather than simple longevity, might be achieved, suggesting that human relationships and meaning will be key to this. He also echoes Vanstone by highlighting waiting and receptivity as being of particular importance:

'Our hearts are restless until they find their rest in Thee.'

Health has this quality of restlessness. It could be that our search for health is the secular mould in which our search for God is cast. We do not find 'God-talk' meaningful, and 'holiness' is sadly devalued. So we speak of our search in a different language, the language of health. But we are betrayed. For our Western conception of health is hollow. We have discerned death as the enemy, but have mistaken its shape. Natural death is the friend of man. We can but stave off his untimely arrival.

But the death of quality, whose shape is meaninglessness,

whose terror is aloneness, and whose sting is dehumanisation, we hardly dare to recognise in ourselves. The splendid weapons of medicine and surgery with which we try to keep death at bay are inappropriate here. They bring us wellness, and for this our appetite is ravenous though perverted. We are already well enough. We exist long enough.

In the struggle for health – for meaning, for community and for fuller humanity – the tools are different. If health is a gift we need not only to strive but also to listen, to bear, to wait, to wonder and to worship. We are what we receive.[39]

Two important issues emerge from this and from what has been explored so far. First, that experiences of health, sickness and death expose our need, as a society, for an alternative language of meaning. In what follows, I will argue that in our contemporary context the word 'spirituality' functions as a catch-all signifier of this largely unarticulated need and explore some of the implications of this. Second, it is clear that while traditional Christian language may have much to offer in this regard, it can no longer *on its own* perform the task of providing a narrative of meaning in a context of meaninglessness. I will therefore address the question of what space there may be for the specificity of Christianity in a world where generic spirituality appears to be the preferred option.

Spirituality and health

First we need to explore in more detail the place of 'spirituality' in contemporary wellbeing agendas, and in order to do that we need to understand a little of where things are at philosophically within current health debates. In a recent discussion paper, Maria Duggan portrays a tension at the heart of current government policies. On the one hand, she says, the English Public Health white paper, *Saving Lives: Our Healthier Nation*, emphasizes the multi-factorial nature of population health and wellbeing. The suggestion is that

health is to a large extent socially and economically constructed, thereby bringing to prominence the need to tackle
health inequalities and to develop wide-ranging interventions
aimed at tackling the root causes of poor health in communities and individuals. The resulting strategy, she argues, has
ushered in a range of new initiatives aiming to improve
health, many of these, including Health and other Action
Zones and Sure Start, 'operationalise a social model of health
and emphasise the need for community development and
empowerment as both a means and an end in health improvement'.

On the other hand, she says,

> at the same time, new health policy is increasingly domi-
> nated [by] what have been called 'scientific-bureaucratic
> approaches' such as clinical governance that emphasise the
> validity of certain kinds of 'hard' scientific investigation
> and intervention over others. The NHS plan . . . has been
> criticised by many analysts for being overly focused on the
> health of the NHS rather than the health of the population.[40]

Duggan's first point can be clearly evidenced by statements
made by the Minister of State for Health when *Our Healthier
Nation* was published. She summed up her philosophy like
this:

> So the new public health is about partnership and mutual
> responsibility at all levels of society and between all levels
> of society – individual, community and national. It is as
> much about wider socio-economic and environmental
> policies as it is about those policies that fall within the port-
> folio of the Department of Health. We now need to think
> very carefully about how we flesh out a new – and critical –
> dimension; psycho-social health.
>
> When ill-defined, it is an approach that is all too easy to
> hold up to mockery, particularly when politicians start to
> write about feelings and emotional well being. However,
> there is no doubt that it is a very serious and important

factor. Too much stress makes you ill. Our ability to cope with stress affects our health. The quality of relationships in society – at home, at work, in the street – is incredibly influential on our health. Socially cohesive societies, where people trust each other, respect each other and are able to say what they feel, are more likely to be healthy societies. Societies where people walk the streets in fear of each other, mutually suspicious and closing off their feelings, are neither happy nor healthy places to be. How people feel – their well being – is an excellent predictor of their physical health.[41]

I want to argue that both of the characteristics of the 'new' health agenda, as outlined by Duggan, provide space for increased attention to issues of 'spirituality'. I will take the first issue first – that is, the multi-factorial nature of health and wellbeing.

A vision for public health which allows that there are dynamics at work other than those encompassed by the inter-relationship of mind and body is most important for 'allowing religion in' to health and social care policy. Conceptual notions that people feel as they do for a complex web of reasons which cannot always be explained in scientific or purely rational terms give rise to attempts to define what this 'other realm' might consist of. In this context 'the spiritual' has begun to emerge as a useful, though far from well-defined, explanatory notion. I will come to the relative advantages and disadvantages of this lack of clarity in due course. For now, it is enough to note how the term is functioning. In her work on religion and mental health, Lynne Friedli also cites a causal link between holistic notions of health and increased interest in issues of religion:

There are a number of developments in public health which are prompting a renewed interest in the relationship between religion and health and suggest that the nature of faith and its consequences for mental wellbeing are impor-tant issues for mental health promotion. A more holistic approach to health is reflected in *Our Healthier Nation*, with its emphasis on the broad social, economic and environmental determinants of health. Partnership and community involvement are central to the success of a wide range of health initiatives, including Health Action Zones, New Commitment to Regeneration and Healthy Living Centres and have stimulated interest in the potential of faith communities as key stakeholders for health.[42]

Much of the resulting discussion on religion/spirituality and health has focused upon the need to see the whole person in thinking about physical and mental health, and therefore upon the need to recognize and address a person's individual 'spiritual needs'. Andrew Solomon, for instance, gives a great deal of space in his book to accounts of people living with depression who have expressed the value to them of religious practice and belief. One of his interviewees talked about evening prayer:

'You get up and say the same prayers every night. Someone has delineated what you're going to say to God and other people say it with you. I'm laying down these rituals to contain my experience. The liturgy is like the wooden slats of a box; the texts of the Bible and especially of the Psalter are considered to be an extremely good box for holding experience. Going to church is a set of attentional practices that move you forward spiritually . . . When I discuss my religious experience with my therapist, or my experience of therapy with my spiritual director, those models turn out to be quite similar. My spiritual director recently told me that the Holy Spirit uses my unconscious all the time! In therapy I learn to erect ego boundaries; in church, I learn to drop them and become one with the universe, or at least part of the body of Christ. I am learning to keep erecting them and dropping them until I can do it like that.' And she snaps her fingers.[43]

The NSF (National Schizophrenia Fellowship), which 'exists

to improve the lives of everyone affected by schizophrenia and other severe mental illnesses by providing quality support, services and information and by influencing local, regional and national policies', has produced a Policy Statement on 'Meeting the spiritual needs of people with a severe mental illness'. This in turn quotes work undertaken by the Mental Health Foundation, whose report *Strategies for Living* (2000) identified some common positive themes arising from the faith and beliefs of service-users:

> Several talked of faith giving them a reason for living at times of despair when suicide might have been an option; many said that they discovered peace through their beliefs; prayer was highly valued by people with religious beliefs [who] found that prayer was of particular value in providing peace and comfort in distress; many sensed God's presence through prayer, through a feeling of unconditional love or that they had the ability to heal.

So the evidence is growing that faith and religious activity can have positive effects for individuals, particularly in terms of mental health. But there is also a corporate and community angle to be explored. An important policy focus for the New Labour years has been that of social capital. Duggan sums up this concept as follows: 'There are many definitions of social capital in use in the literature. The concept involves social relationships, social support, formal and informal social networks, group membership, shared norms, trust, reciprocity and community and civic engagement.'[44] Increasing social capital has been shown to improve public health. This means that activities that encourage social networking and collaborative community-based efforts are positively regarded in the contemporary public health agenda.

Suddenly, many of those mundane social activities undertaken by Christian communities and other faith groups can be seen in a new light: coffee mornings, drop-ins, luncheon clubs for older people, shoppers' cafes in the High Street, parent and toddler groups, Sunday school, youth clubs – even the Ladies' Bright Hour – can be rebranded in our contemporary context as promoting social cohesion and therefore having health-promoting potential. In an individualistic and atomized society, the political rediscovery of the concept of 'society' and 'community' puts faith groups in a strong position to be, in Friedli's words, 'key stakeholders for health' – simply by doing what they have always done.

Of course, many within the Christian community and other faith communities are not simply doing what they have always done. Building on the opportunities made possible by the emphasis on partnership working as outlined by Tessa Jowell above, many churches are seizing the opportunity to deliver new, innovative and imaginative services to those who need them most. The Sainsbury Centre for Mental Health has produced a publication entitled 'On Your Doorstep: Community Organisations and Mental Health'.[45] This report focuses on two projects as case studies: the Bromley-by-Bow Healthy Living Centre in East London and the Health First Action project in West Earlham, Norwich. Both projects have significant church involvement, and they are but two of many examples of initiatives across the country that could have been chosen. New possibilities abound at the present time for faith communities to contribute to the theory and practice of public health development.

Let us now return to the second characteristic of the contemporary health scene identified by Duggan – those 'scientific-bureaucratic approaches'. Measurable and monitored outcomes and targets are, of course, a necessary part of public accountability and for that reason should be defended. There is, however, a growing unease with a perceived obsession with 'the measurable'. Not least when there appear always to be ways to massage figures to create an impression that things are better or worse than they are, depending upon which is necessary to gain increased funds. Ironically, though, the very attempt to make everything quantifiable somehow highlights the fact that, in the end, there is much of value that cannot be so measured. The creation of ever more complex benchmarks and performance indicators serves only to make it increasingly obvious that human experience cannot be comprehensively embraced in this way – however excellently the scientific methodology is executed.

For instance, academics have struggled hard to measure the impact on human health of the foot-and-mouth crisis. The focus has been on indicators such as the frequency of visits to the GP by those resident in affected areas, and increases in suicide rates. There are many valuable lessons to be learned from such research. But two facts remain: first, that the indicators used are based upon knowledge that we already have or best-guess assumptions as to what might be the case, and, second, that however many of them are chosen, they remain merely blunt instruments for assessing a multi-factorial phenomenon which can never be pinned down. To make good these limitations, there is a tendency to fall back on so-called 'qualitative data' or 'anecdotal evidence'. This often takes the form of real quotes from real people about their experience of, for example, living with foot-and-mouth disease. While usually considered to be of secondary importance, such qualitative data is the real site of new learning. It is from this that we gain, for example, insight into: the complexity of the psychological impact upon both rural and urban dwellers of restricted access to the countryside (can we measure the stress-relieving effects of looking at the colour green?); the effect on farm-dwellers of being holed up and isolated from the rest of society for weeks on end; the feelings of delivery-people at having to go through the dehumanizing process of being hosed down with disinfectant several times a day; the sadness felt by farmers and vets as they had to slaughter animals or leave them uncared for in the fields against a lifetime's instincts of animal husbandry; or their despair at yet another economic disaster to make life apparently not worth living. There is little that can be simply benchmarked or measured here, yet these are the life experiences which, more than anything else, cause us to ask serious meaning-of-life questions. 'Spiritual' questions spring from what cannot be measured and, paradoxically, the trend towards measuring everything highlights the need to find other ways for things to matter.

Assessing spirituality

Various conclusions have so far been drawn about how the term 'spirituality' is functioning in contemporary health care debates. The most important observation is that it is becoming increasingly important. As Stephen Pattison, in an article written with John Swinton, has said:

> At a time when formal religious observance is diminishing in the UK, interest is growing among healthcare professionals in matters religious and spiritual. New-age and complementary therapies are flourishing, the number of NHS chaplains has more than doubled, and there is interest in the spiritual duties of healthcare staff, particularly nurses, in relation to patient care.[46]

We have seen how spirituality represents an important component in the increasingly popular holistic emphasis in health – both in terms of individual needs and those of the communities to which individuals belong. We have also seen how spirituality offers the possibility of a new language of meaning which gives a thicker and fuller account of human well-being and an alternative perspective on what matters which goes beyond materialistic considerations.

Various attempts have been made to define and pin down 'the spiritual' in order to facilitate policy-making in this arena, but clarity has so far proved elusive. Rabbi Julia Neuberger has summed up the difficulties as follows:

> Is 'spirituality' that sense of 'the other' we heard so many people describe at the time of the death of Princess Diana? Is it somewhat mawkish and sentimental, ill thought through – but 'a good thing' all the same? Does it fit with groups of young women sitting on the grass at Kensington Gardens, meditating around a candle, with masses of flowers? Or is it more to do with the angry coming to terms with the impending death of the terminally ill person who

recognises she has not got long to go? Or is it the mood of calm engendered by communion brought to the bedside, or the lighting of Sabbath candles? Or is it all of these things?[47]

Let us explore some of the other definitions that have been offered. The aforementioned NSF Policy Statement 40, 'Meeting the spiritual needs of people with a severe mental illness', deploys a definition used by the Brighton and South Downs NHS Trust, attributed to Murray and Zentner (1986):

> It's a quality that goes beyond religious affiliation, that strives for inspiration, reverence, awe, meaning and purpose, even in those who do not believe in any god. The spiritual dimension tries to be in harmony with the universe, strives for answers about the infinite and comes into focus when a person faces emotional illness, physical illness and death.

David Lyall turns to the nursing literature for help. He discovers Linda Ross who has 'defined the spiritual dimension as "that element within the individual from which originates: meaning, purpose and fulfilment in life; a will to live; belief and faith in self, others and God and which is essential to the attainment of an optimum state of health, wellbeing or quality of life'. Another author cited by David Lyall speaks of spirituality as being characterized by 'interconnectedness and self-transcendence'.[48]

Stephen Pattison, more than any other theologian, has given systematic attention to analysing the development of the concept of spirituality in health care contexts. I will be using his acute and timely observations extensively in what follows. For starters, he and John Swinton write:

> 'Spirituality' is often used as a more inclusive substitute for the word religion. Definitions are various, fluid and imprecise. Spirituality can be understood as that aspect of human existence which relates to structures of significance that gives meaning and direction to a person's life and helps

them deal with the vicissitudes of existence. It is associated with the human quest for meaning, purpose, self-transcending knowledge, meaningful relationships, love and a sense of the holy. It may, or may not, be associated with a specific religious system.[49]

Spirituality, then, is to be understood as distinct from and going beyond organized and institutionalized religious systems and traditions. Belief in God is not necessary to it, though *belief itself* is, but this can encompass a variety of things: belief in the harmony of the universe; in the possibility of self-transcendence; in meaningful relationships; in a meaning and purpose to life. Spirituality is variously perceived as essential to optimum wellbeing, or as that which comes into focus mainly at times of crisis. In his characteristically caustic style, Pattison sums up the functioning of the concept as follows:

Notions of 'spirituality' that are presently in play are diffuse, vague and contradictory. 'Spirituality' seems to function like intellectual polyfilla, changing shape and content conveniently to fill the space its users devise for it. Having mostly departed from the theories and practices of religion, theorists and practitioners of spirituality are muddled about what actually constitutes their subject matter.[50]

The question is, does this muddle matter? I would argue that it does, and for two reasons.

A fascinating article appeared in the *Health Service Journal* on 23 August 2001, looking at how staff in homes for the care of elderly people understand the concept of 'meeting the spiritual needs' of those in their care.[51] A postal survey asked home managers which of the following eight specified activities they considered to involve 'spiritual care': saying a prayer with a resident when asked to do so; taking the residents on a trip to the countryside; arranging for the local school to come and sing Christmas carols; comforting a resident who is worried about continence issues; ensuring a resident sees their favourite TV programme; reading a resident an old letter they particularly treasure; discussing with a resident their funeral wishes; listening while a resident reminisces about their spouse.

The responses to this survey showed that more than half the managers considered all these activities to be spiritual care. Results were particularly high for saying a prayer with a resident, discussing funeral arrangements (both 90 per cent), and reading letters and listening to reminiscences.

The authors surveyed all residential and nursing homes in the Trent region – some 1,500 in all. They achieved a 42 per cent reply rate – 644 homes, encompassing all types, sizes and locations of homes in the sector. The results, according to the authors, 'point towards a broad, all-encompassing perception of spirituality on the part of home managers'.[52] They comment:

> While it is hardly surprising that items with religious connotations ranked highly, tasks connected with relationships and remembrance also featured strongly. In addition, comforting a resident worried about continence – an emotional issue of an intimate personal nature, but without any overt connection with spirituality – was also considered to have a spiritual dimension by 60 per cent of managers.[53]

Given the ground so far explored in this chapter, these results will come as no surprise. More interesting, however, were the responses to the question of whose responsibility it is to meet the needs associated with such a broad and all-encompassing concept of spirituality. Here, the authors reported a great deal of confusion. Some said that it was the responsibility of all staff, others that it was the role of senior staff. Others saw a role for external religious leaders, and some even considered it the responsibility of those staff who themselves had a religious faith. Thereby suggesting, as the authors point out, 'a misunderstanding in what is involved in providing spiritual care, with a reversion to a traditional understanding that links it closely with religion'.[54] Overall, the conclusion is:

The comments of many managers indicated that, despite the increased profile of spiritual care, it is still something of a taboo area and one which staff often find embarrassing. Access to appropriate training and education was a common concern for home managers. It is clear that training which provides basic facts, dispels myths and helps staff to explore boundaries is a key component in enabling those who work in this environment to meet better the needs of the significant numbers of older people living in the residential sector.[55]

This article highlights the practical difficulties in implementing policies associated with vague and slippery notions of spirituality. It is Government policy, as expressed in the National Service Framework for Older People, that spiritual needs must be met as part of end-of-life care. Though it may be philosophically pleasing, in the abstract, to see spirituality everywhere and in everything, such a perspective is hardly a firm foundation for transforming practice at the sharp end of service delivery. There is a huge awareness-raising, training and research agenda here. Not least because, as the *HSJ* article points out,

> Younger staff seemed to find this area particularly difficult . . . Young staff rarely had much exposure to structured religious belief systems in the way that would have been common just 50 years ago. They may have a schoolbook knowledge of the major religions, but little familiarity with the basic currency of religious expression – rites, rituals and terminology.[56]

As Stephen Pattison and John Swinton have said, 'While there is clear evidence that religion is often a positive force for health, more research is needed – in particular into the effects of different religious traditions on health and wellbeing; ways in which spirituality and religion affect people's lives . . . [and] how the health service might deal more effectively with these dimensions in the lives of service users.'[57]

As I suggested earlier, there is a second danger in vague and undefined notions of spirituality. Again it is Pattison who identifies it through his keen observations about what the term has come to mean: 'spirituality is an unequivocally "good thing". It is universally valid and valued. Everyone does and should have "it", and because they do, they should have the spiritual needs, however defined, met. There appears to be no such thing as a dubious spirituality, a harmful spirituality, or one that should not be indulged.'[58] Anyone with more than a glancing familiarity with spiritual and religious belief systems knows that – as I said in my introduction – they have the potential to make people sick: to do harm as well as good. All spiritual and religious beliefs have some accompanying human organizational authority structure, however informal (indeed, the gravest damage can often be done through informal rather than formal authority structures). Any such structure provides a potential platform for abuse: financial exploitation; physical, emotional and sexual abuse and manipulation; damaging forms of authoritarianism; and beliefs which undermine the personal identity and integrity of adherents. All are the possible outworkings of religious and spiritual belief systems, and Pattison is right to draw our attention to the dangers of a lack of critical analysis in this area.

There is undoubtedly a difficult collection of issues here, particularly in our contemporary multi-cultural context where religious and spiritual identity is often inextricably linked with racial and cultural identity. But a policy of simply and uncritically 'respecting someone's beliefs and meeting their spiritual needs', whatever they are perceived to be, will not best serve the interests of human equality, diversity and flourishing. Much health-damaging gender and sexuality discrimination, for instance, is defended on the grounds that it is simply part of a religious belief system. Though it is customary to notice this only when it is carried out within minority ethnic communities, it is worth pointing out that the most common examples of such discrimination in Britain today are those perpetrated by mainstream Christian organizations.

Institutionalized sexism within the Church of England, for example, disqualifies women from its highest offices, and leaders from a range of Christian organizations have in recent years argued for exemption from the Human Rights Act on the grounds that discriminatory practices are sometimes justified for religious reasons.

Understanding what is harmful and what is helpful in spirituality and religion is a complex and value-laden exercise. All the more reason to begin amassing our knowledge and developing our tools for critical analysis *now*. In this task it is likely that those who understand the territory and texture of spirituality, as broadly defined, and religious belief systems more narrowly, have more to offer than those for whom all of this holds little meaning or attraction. To be rooted in one tradition limits one's vision, but it simultaneously expands it too. I believe, therefore, that there is a clear role for Christians here – alongside those of other faith traditions and of none. The trap to avoid, for all those involved in this conversation, is the assumption that a religious or spiritual tradition is helpful *by definition*, simply because it is one's own.

A theological assessment of notions of spirituality inevitably forces us to focus on the relationship between spirituality and theology. Theologian Daniel Hardy observes: 'To an astonishing extent, the relation between spirituality and theology has become pivotal for religious practice and its intersection with wider concerns.' As we have seen, this is certainly true in the case of health and wellbeing. Hardy goes on to say: 'Large numbers of people now treat spirituality as central to human concerns, where theology often appears to have lost its position as normative for human life. One reason is that "spirituality" has become a haven for those who have, for various reasons, freed themselves from conventional religious practice and its underpinnings in "theology".'[59] I would venture to suggest that another reason is that those responsible for communicating theological ideas have not taken seriously enough the need to find appropriate ways to make themselves accessible and understood in our complex cultural climate, but I'll come to that shortly.

Hospital chaplains are one professional group that lives and works very much at the interface between the spiritual and the theological. By way of a case study, let us explore for a moment what is at stake for them at this point in time. Much space is given to precisely these issues in the book *Spirituality in Health Care Contexts*.[60] Two contributors in particular focus upon them. Echoing Hardy's themes, David Lyall says:

> The context of contemporary chaplaincy is precisely this tension between contemporary 'Humanistic' understandings of spirituality and more traditional Christian approaches. I want to argue that within this context, the key issues in hospital chaplaincy relate to identity and integrity. There is undoubtedly much disillusionment with institutional religion and we must be sensitive to that. There is also growing evidence of the reality of religious experience as evidenced in the research of David Hay and Kate Hunt (2000). They have demonstrated in their 'Soul of Britain' survey that 76 per cent of the population admit to some kind of spiritual experience (a huge positive response compared with 25 years ago).[61]

I will return to his themes of identity and integrity shortly.

The other key contributor, almost inevitably, is Stephen Pattison, who muses:

> If 'spirituality' in general terms is more desirable than religion, it is unclear what part representatives of religious communities should play in delivering 'spiritual care'. Indeed, it is precisely because of their specifically religious origins and training that chaplains as representatives of particular religious views and communities may be the last people suitable for facilitating or providing 'spiritual care' in the generic, secularised sense that seems now to be prevalent across a variety of professions.[62]

Into this context of acute and creative self-questioning speak the insights of a practical initiative in Newham, East London.

This is a project which has been written up in two publications from the Sainsbury Centre for Mental Health: *Keeping Faith: The Provision of Community Health Services within a Multi-faith Context* (1997) and *Forward in Faith: An Experiment in Building Bridges between Ethnic Communities and Mental Health Services in East London* (2001). Both are by Nigel Copsey.

He sketches for us the characteristics of the neighbourhood in which this particular mental health project is set. London's East End, he reminds us, is now the most ethnically diverse area in the UK. In Newham it is estimated that over 50 per cent of the population belong to minority ethnic communities. It is one of the most deprived boroughs in the UK and includes a large number of asylum-seekers. Copsey emphasizes the importance of religion in this part of London when he says, 'There are over 75 Hindu groups, over 20 mosques and some 4 gurdwaras. And there are 24 other religious groups . . . Probably at least 40% of the population of Newham has contact with a faith group of some sort . . . Therefore faith communities form the most significant group within the local population.'[63]

In the second of the two publications, he summarizes the project in the following way:

> Over the past two years, a new department for spiritual, religious and cultural care within mental health services has been established in the London Borough of Newham . . . we have developed a model of care that meets the diverse faith needs of our local communities, rather than simply apply-ing the conventional chaplaincy model. I am even more convinced now than I was two years ago that the decision to move away from the traditional model was the right one.[64]

By way of a brief summary, the model has involved appoint-ing a 'co-ordinator of religious, spiritual and cultural care' rather than a chaplain. The co-ordinator's job has been to establish and maintain strong links with the diverse faith com-munities in Newham, while at the same time building strong relationships with mental health service staff. The aim has been to ensure that service-users have their faith understood so that they feel supported during their treatment. The model is constantly developing: 'The team now consists of three co-ordinators and two multilingual co-workers. We reflect the community of Newham culturally and religiously, combining our resources to respond to local communities.'[65] The initial focus has been the establishment of a structure for pastoral care on the acute wards and day hospital. But, as Copsey says, 'Our aim was to begin at this point of entry and then to move outwards.'[66] The subsequent focus upon preventive work within the community has been enabled through a well-resourced and trained team of volunteers.

While the spiritual needs of the population of Newham are conspicuously diverse, I would argue that such variety is a characteristic of every part of Britain, though in many places this diversity is hidden. There may not everywhere be significant numbers of adherents to a range of commonly recognized major faith traditions, but – according to the wider definition of spirituality explored so far – there will certainly be a diversity of spiritual needs. In such a context, is there a role at all for Christian chaplains? And if so, what is it? Pattison reinforces this question sharply:

> So what are chaplains . . . of a specific tradition supposed to do with their religious roots and perceptions? Are they to leave their origins, rituals, teachings and traditions behind? Should they regard them as an optional resource for those who can make use of 'that kind of thing' while trying to act as spiritual guides and mentors of all, religious or not?[67]

It seems to me that Copsey's model blows apart the dichotomy implied by Pattison in the earlier quote and reinforced above – that is, between serving 'specific religious traditions' and 'generic spirituality'. It feels as though the choice, as presented by Pattison, is between the so-called traditional chaplaincy model (presumably a white middle-aged Anglican cleric dispensing specifically Christian services to those who tick a box claiming to be 'Church of England' and anyone else who cares to join in), and the same person rushing around desperately trying to be 'all spiritual things to all people'. The Newham model offers, dare I say it, a third way. That is, the use of *generic skills* (of co-ordination, facilitation, education) to enhance the access of all service-users to the *specific spiritual resources* they feel they need. In this schema, chaplains – and others in Christian ministry – become simply part of a wider team, each member of which offers what is specific to their own spiritual tradition.

I would now like to move beyond the case study of hospital chaplaincy to look more widely at the interface between church and society. I think the distinction made above between 'generic skills' and 'specific spiritual resources' is a useful one in helping us to gain some clarity about what is perceived to be a difference between spirituality and theology. One comment from David Lyall about chaplaincy is a useful jumping-off point. He concludes:

> At the end of the day, in the midst of the complexity of contemporary spirituality, individual and institutional, and all that passes for religion, good and bad, chaplains can only be who they are, representatives of a eucharistic, story-formed community. To be otherwise is simply to reflect the fragmentation of contemporary society and religion and be of little use to the hospital as institution.[68]

Insofar as he is referring to 'specific spiritual resources' he is probably right. As Stephen Pattison has said, it would be inappropriate for Christian clergy to attempt to become 'brokers of spirituality in all its manifestations from Wicca to Buddhism'.[69] But it is my contention that Lyall's focus on the *content of Christian belief* causes him to miss the potential contribution that can be made in terms of 'generic skills'.

My argument applies, potentially, to all representatives of the Christian community, lay and ordained, and not just chaplains. But in order to further illustrate what I mean, I will focus on the role of clergy. I suggest that, at best, they possess a range of generic and transferable 'spiritual skills' that they sometimes don't realize they have and certainly don't value highly enough. The reason that clergy don't realize they have these generic skills is that they rarely exercise them outside of what Lyall calls 'the story-formed community' of the church. Because clergy are under pressure (for a variety of reasons too complicated to go into here) to operate almost exclusively within the club, these generic skills are seen as merely 'specific spiritual resources' when they are, in fact, more than that.

Some concrete examples will help. Liturgy can be considered as a purely Christian activity. Worship is the very focus of the 'eucharistic, story-formed community'. Yet seen in another way, it is so much more than that. Those who are well practised in the design of worship and liturgy could also be seen as being gifted with a rare generic skill: the use of the language of ritual to create dramatic and moving forms of expression which enable the articulation of truths which cannot be articulated in any other way. As we have already seen in this book, the use of ritual and the deployment of 'the symbolic' are an enormously important resource for building emotional resilience and health, both for individuals and communities. Who else in our society besides those who are rooted in story-formed communities where ritual is central can bring those gifts to the communal table? Who else has developed these skills in a systematic way, with intellectual underpinning? Who else has centuries of 'good-practice' models to draw on?

Preaching and theological reflection is another example. The fact that this most often involves propounding a specifically Christian message to a bunch of self-identified church people does not alter the fact that it could also be seen as a more widely applicable discursive genre for talking about the enduring human themes of meaning, life, death and change. Wedding and funeral sermons are, I suppose, one context in which clergy are already adept at communicating the things that matter in a language which is less christo-centric than is the norm for Sunday worship. In short, I believe that the churches have enormous riches here to offer to a society obviously hungry for spiritual and religious expression, but unsure how to access it. The Christian community could be offering so much more than it is, if only it could break through what appears to be a massive language barrier. The question is: when is it appropriate for Christians to use our generic skills without necessarily giving a high profile to the christocentric content which usually accompanies the deployment of them? In exploring this question, we are returned to David Lyall's original key themes of identity and integrity.

A common-sense assumption abounds among Christians that to speak at all times and in all places with the language of the story-formed community of the church is what it means to witness to Christian truth. This assumption needs to be challenged. The key considerations, surely, are: for whose benefit are we communicating at all, and for what purpose? The evangelist who shouts at passers-by in the high street is not communicating in the interests of his audience. Indeed, he (for it is usually a he) is arguably not really communicating at all. He is acting on his own behalf, to make himself feel better about his personal relationship with God. But his communication does absolutely nothing for those it is directed at.

Representatives of the Christian community – not least spiritual leaders – often find themselves in circumstances where, in order to make sense and have credibility, they must adopt the language of their context to communicate ideas which they would normally choose to address in a more explicitly 'Christian' way. For instance, many bishops are taking on roles in Regeneration Partnerships in major cities in this country. Often they are seen as 'honest brokers' – bringing together private, statutory and voluntary sectors while themselves preserving a measure of independence from all three. They take on such roles, quite rightly, because they are representatives of an institution and of a faith tradition which prioritizes the needs of the marginalized and excluded in society. Regeneration initiatives are an important way, in the current climate, to do just that. I assume, however, that such bishops do not expect to begin Regeneration Partnership meetings with a prayer, as they would their own diocesan synods. And I assume also that when they proffer opinions about socio-economic complexities, they do not prefigure their contributions with the words of Jesus, or of Paul, ever-present as these words may be in their own minds.

But it is not just spiritual leaders who deploy language in this way. Ordinary lay members of churches have this experience daily: at work, at play and in interpersonal relationships. They face the challenge of communicating ideas and convictions which are religiously inspired in ways which others will find meaningful, and this often involves making no explicit reference to Christianity at all. Many lay people express frustration that their life from Monday to Saturday is not recognized or valued in their church life, and I'm sure that this is, in part at least, related to this language issue. They feel 'dichotomized' by the fact that the language of the church and the language of the world often seem to have no connection with one another. This language barrier makes lay people feel that they are being two different people, not one integrated spiritual person who also has a life outside church.

Many Christians worry that to speak in a language other than the internal christocentric language used at church is somehow to be involved in compromise or to sell the Christian message short. It is my concluding perspective in this book that, in the intersection of church and society, untangling the generic from the christocentric is something that religious believers (all of them, not just clergy) need to be more self-conscious about, and better at. We all need to improve our ability self-consciously to deploy different languages according to circumstances. Sometimes to speak christocentric language in non-Christian contexts can be entirely appropriate. But most of the time it will be pointless. We have entered a polyglot spiritual universe. The new world is one where the skills most at a premium are those of trans-lation.

Novelist Jeanette Winterson has said:

The artist is a translator; one who has learned how to pass into her own language the languages gathered from stones, from birds, from dreams, from the body, from the material world, from the invisible world, from sex, from death, from love. A different language is a different reality; what is the language, the world, of stones? What is the language, the world, of birds? Of atoms? Of microbes? Of colours? Of air?[70]

I think there is a parallel between a religious person and an artist. For the Christian, for instance, the question is: how to pass into the secular world the insights of one's Christian heritage? How to tell the Christian story in that context? But also, crucially, the question must be put the other way around: how to pass back into the corporate christocentric language of the church the insights of the other languages used in our everyday life? According to this linguistic model, one's Christian identity stands to be transformed by one's secular identity and vice versa.

I have deployed elsewhere in this book Eva Hoffman's *Lost in Translation*. This work is a wonderfully rich exploration of how language shapes and determines the complexity of human identity. Having lived in Poland during the formative years of her childhood, Hoffman emigrated with her parents to Canada before she reached adolescence. Her book is an account of her life from childhood to adulthood, and in its focus on translation as the process by which identity gets changed and renegotiated it offers helpful analytical tools for our current discussion.

She speaks, for instance, of the temptation to isolate herself from her new world, and to attempt simply to retain her 'Polishness' against all odds. She discovers, of course, that this is a lonely and, in the long-term, an unrealistic option. But having decided that interaction with her new culture is necessary and inevitable, the next question is how to negotiate this contact. How to do this without obliterating the former self? As she puts it:

The soul can shrivel from an excess of critical distance, and if I don't want to remain in arid internal exile for the rest of my life, I have to find a way to lose my alienation without losing my self. But how does one bend toward another culture without falling over, how does one strike an elastic balance between rigidity and self-effacement?[71]

The religious parallels are obvious. Sometimes religious people and traditions aim to keep themselves separate from the world around them. They aim for purity and distinctiveness. Alienation, for followers of such traditions, is a way of life – even a virtue. But most of us don't want that, and don't see it as the Christian calling. The question then, however, is how to strike that balance between rigidity in our faith traditions, and their obliteration or effacement?

This is Hoffman's conclusion:

I have to make a shift in the innermost ways. I have to *translate myself*. But if I'm to achieve this without becoming assimilated – that is, absorbed – by my new world, the translation has to be careful, the turns of the psyche unforced. To mouth foreign terms without incorporating their meanings is to risk becoming bowdlerized. A true translation proceeds by the motions of understanding and sympathy; it happens by slow increments, sentence by sentence, phrase by phrase.[72] (italics mine)

What Hoffman highlights in her reflections is the need to inhabit, potentially, several realities at once. Human identity, particularly in our fragmented world, is complex and multiple. It is helpful to conceptualize this according to a linguistic model – as Hoffman does when she says, 'Like everybody, I am the sum of my languages – the language of my family and childhood, and education and friendship, and love, and the larger, changing world – though perhaps I tend to be more aware than most of the fractures between them.'[73] We see, therefore, that the best way to negotiate our complex identities is by allowing each reality to retain its own identity and integrity, while also enabling its interaction with the others through translation: a slow and painstaking process.

A crucial point, however, is that the translation process changes and profoundly affects all of the realities which are being negotiated. In Hoffman's words there is no chance of returning, in any of the languages we speak, to a 'point of origin'. As she says of her 'Polishness':

> Experience creates style, and style, in turn, creates a new woman. Polish is no longer the one, true language against which others live their secondary life. Polish insights cannot be regained in their purity; there's something I know in English too. The wholeness of childhood truths is inter-mingled with the divisiveness of adult doubt. When I speak Polish now, it is infiltrated, permeated, and inflected by the English in my head. Each language modifies the other, crossbreeds with it, fertilizes it. Each language makes the other relative.[74]

To return to the parallel with religion, Christians are not simply members of 'a eucharistic, story-formed community', though that is part of who we are. We are, simultaneously, members of the wider community within which the Christian community is set. We speak a multitude of languages according to our age, ethnicity, class, gender, set of friends, educational background, career choice, physical and psychological constitution, etc. The interaction between church and society is a linguistic interaction between individuals and institutions as they translate meaning back and forth. In the process, both society and church are changed and, crucially, it is not possible to say which of these is the 'point of origin'. For Christians to be effective in such linguistic encounters, two things are necessary. First, we need to be able to speak our own language articulately and effectively, and, second, we need to develop 'the motions of understanding and sympathy' with the secular world around us in order to become good translators.

Using our underlying theme of health and wellbeing may help to clarify what I mean here. In order to interact effectively with secular agendas in this field, churches need constantly to be working out our specifically Christian understandings of, for instance: God's call to life in all its fullness; the meaning of gospel imperatives to heal the sick and support those in need; the implications of the biblical vision that each and every human being is unique and of infinite equal value to God. Alongside this, however, there is a need to translate the insights of this internal debate into the secular language of the wider world. But to do so in such a way that something new is added to that debate which changes it, and something is taken away from the debate which in turn alters our Christian assumptions and insights.

It is often assumed that Christian truths are fixed and stable. They determine who we are and what message we will deliver to the world. I am arguing here for a more dynamic model. My vision of the Christian identity is that it is not simply the *foundation*, the jumping-off point, for our activity. It is also the *product* of our activity. We may undertake certain activities because of our Christian identity but in undertaking these, the nature of our Christian identity changes. We see new visions of God and of humanity, and have to reconceptualize our faith accordingly. Identity and experience are locked in a mutually enhancing cycle – changed by one another. In the encounter between church and society, the trick is to ensure that Christianity is neither lost in translation, nor left unaffected by it.

MIRACLES?

On religion: a parable

My name is Miracle and in many ways, I suppose, that's what I am. I shouldn't be here at all, according to my mother. I was born too early, you see. Three months too early, to be precise. Tiny being that I was when I slipped out, not yet fully formed, I should never have been viable outside the womb.

My life then was a fight against the seemingly foregone conclusion of death. My life now is, according to my mother at least, a testament to divine intervention. She prayed for my life. I battled for it. Doctors and nurses worked overtime. God got the credit. But let's not quibble. The point is that this is my story. *This is the stuff of miracles*.

I work in a café at Victoria station in central London. Sometimes it feels like the busiest place in the world. I see people. I see fortunes made and lost, deals done and broken, decisions made and minds changed. I catch glimpses of exhilaration and utter despair. I see hatred and frustration, joy and temptation, tenderness, determination, spontaneity, nervousness and restraint, recklessness and abandon, caution and regret. And I know that *this is the stuff of miracles*.

More than anything, I see love. There is new love. 'This is who I am and this is what my life means.' So say new lovers, one to another, in my café, before their trains leave, before my very eyes. And in the saying of it, the meaning of their lives changes. Who they are changes through who they are becoming to one another. From where I'm standing, new loves look strange and dangerous. Taking the risk promises everything or nothing.

But old love can be dangerous too – when it's between those who feel that the way things are is simply the ways things must be. Not that old love is necessarily like that. I've seen it at its most beautiful, with the challenge still built in; where surprise is possible and change is a friend. Often I see people who are suspended between old love and new love and don't know where to put themselves. Sometimes it feels as though the whole universe is poised between the old and the new, forced into an impossible choice between delicious disruption and life-giving stability. And, believe me, the whole universe passes through here. I feel that what I'm watching is sacramental. *This is the stuff of miracles.*

I'm not actually from here. I'm from a palace. More of that later. I don't belong amid this hectic mass of constant change. I'm from the hills, where change is slower. City people are funny about the countryside. They think it's pure. They think that nature is elemental – spiritual, untouched by human hands. But to the trained eye the nips and tucks of years of land management are etched into the body that we call the land. In a way, people are as present there as they are in my café. It's just that the gaps between them are bigger. My meaning is found in the people, but also in the gaps between them.

On a bad day in the hills, when the vastness of the landscape becomes an audible taunt to my smallness, I recall the people who have grown me. And on a bad day in the city, when the people are so many that their bodies melt to liquid irritation, I play in my mind with fragments of remembered yellow fields. Wherever I am, I am in the realm of what earth has given and human hands have made. *This is the stuff of miracles.*

I was born in 1974, one of five bishop's daughters. The youngest and the smallest. Born into a palace, grand but neglected. Born out of the will of others that I should survive. Borne up by their instinct that I was worth it.

The language of my childhood was the language of 'just enough'. Just enough time to head off accusations of parental neglect; just enough money to err on the comfortable side of ascetic; just enough love to plant the all-important seed of self-assurance; just enough talk to learn to express important things and to make enough room in my soul for the unsaid crucial things.

Any extravagance was saved for God. His was the realm of contagious self-giving; the land of feasting and abundance; the promise of goodness pressed down, shaken together, overflowing; the prospect of tongues loosed and lives liberated. But looking around me at church, as I often did, I couldn't help but wonder why everyone looked so depleted by this divine economy of grace. And I still wonder, why do believers look like so many screwed-up and crumpled sermon notes, cast aside in favour of bigger and better ideas? *Is this the stuff of miracles?*

God was with us. At the rising of the sun we hailed him: 'O Lord our heavenly Father, Almighty and everlasting God, who hast safely brought us to the beginning of this day: defend us with thy mighty power and grant that this day we fall into no sin, neither run into any kind of danger...'

And at the going down of the same, we bid him goodnight: 'O God, from whom all desires, all good counsels and all just works do proceed: give unto thy servants that peace which the world cannot give ... Lighten our darkness we beseech thee, O Lord; and by thy great mercy defend us from all perils and dangers of this night ...'

My life was structured by ritual, punctuated by sacrament. Its rhythm was the rhythm of my life. Its beauty was my way into all beauty; its language my way into all ways of making sense. The words are still magic to me. Religion, for me, has never been an option. I am it. It is me. I can't stop being it without stopping being, and I don't know how to do that. *This is the stuff of miracles.*

My friends loved our place, our palace. So many sites of play and exploration. My life had an exotic fairy-tale quality. They found it hard to believe that bishops still existed. And I too remember the fascinating revelation that everyone's life was not like mine. It was utterly astounding to me that there were households without the shape of 'God' in every nook and cranny – the invisible imaginary friend. As astounding as discovering that one of my friends had no books in her house. No books!

Friends, in turn, were baffled by me. What's it like, they'd say, having God in your house? When I knew no alternative, I couldn't answer the question.

Now I can venture to say that this is how it was: it was like living by a corporate mission statement that was never explained but always assumed; it was like living with a riddle that you had to work out backwards from the clues. The clues were a random rag-bag collection of childish things: it's not OK to play out on Sundays; you have to go to church, even when you're on holiday; if a tramp comes to the door, you feed him; if the phone rings, you always answer it; life is work and work is life; you always put yourself last; you work hardest when everyone else is on holiday; there are no weekends, no 'out of hours'; when somebody dies, it's normal. But it was also knowing that whatever you did, you were special; however you did, you were loved. *This was the stuff of miracles.*

One day my father went out to empty the bins, and was killed by a slate that was blown from the palace roof by a freak gust of wind. Nobody imagines bishops putting out the rubbish, but they have to, just like anyone else. The slate that pierced his heart sliced through my own life also. Truncated my childhood. And we were moved out of the palace: a new race – fatherless and widowed. And the shape of God as I had known it remained in every nook and cranny – of the palace. It became precisely that which God was not supposed to be: limited to time and place and circumstance. People are my religion now. Love is my meaning. *Is this the stuff of miracles?*

Sometimes I'm asked what I remember most about my father, and I have to say that I remember his hands. Celebrating the Eucharist. My father's hands were expert hands – most deft in the delivery of sacrament. I used to love to watch them. So familiar, those hands that once were larger than my own back, which between them enclosed me perfectly, now performing miracles with bread and wine. They came alive in the doing of this. He comes alive through my memory of it. *This is the stuff of miracles.*

People say I'm not religious any more. They may be right, but their evidence is slender. They know that I no longer frequent church rituals, but they don't know why I don't. The real reason is not as it seems. They think I think them insignificant, but the opposite is the case.

Curiously, I follow in my father's footsteps. I'm an expert performer now. You should see me with my coffee machines. It's not easy making espresso and cappuccino, you know. How many bad coffees have you tasted? My coffee is made with love.

People think change is hard, but I'm not so sure. I've seen transformation for the price of a cappuccino. Take my friend Ruth. There she was one day, waiting outside the café. Except she wasn't my friend then, she was a stranger. She was waiting for someone who never showed up. She sat for a couple of hours – just waiting. Whoever was to come was obviously bringing the answers to her life, for when they failed to come, it seemed as though she suddenly had no life. It was strangely awesome to see her change. I saw her eyes as anticipation turned to concern, concern to fear, and fear to a most terrifying emptiness. There she was – small and bleached of hope. Sitting in the doorway of my café.

I was apprehensive. I wanted to do something, but I didn't know what. This could be the last straw for her, I thought. I've seen last straws before, I know what they look like. I learned later that Ruth was running away. Anyway, I took her a cappuccino. 'Here's a coffee,' I said, 'I made it for you.' She looked at me for a long while, then took it. Later, she said that the acceptance of that cappuccino was a choice as hard as any she had ever made. For to take it was to start again, to believe again in the possibility of trust. To refuse would have been the death of her, she said. To accept it was a resurrection. *This is the stuff of miracles.*

Religion and wellbeing

Theologian Rowan Williams was in New York on 11 September 2001 – a couple of blocks away from the World Trade Center when the planes hit. He was on site as the events of that day unfolded. Reflecting later on this life-changing experience, he wrote a little book, *Writing in the Dust:*

Reflections on 11th September and its Aftermath. In this he high-lights what he calls 'a frightening contrast' between 'the murderously spiritual' and 'the compassionately secular'.[1] The inspiration for his reflection came from the mobile phone calls made to loved ones by those caught up in the tragedy who knew they were going to die. He says this:

> Someone who is about to die in terrible anguish makes room in their mind for someone else; for the grief and terror of someone they love. They do what they can to take some atom of that pain away from the other by the inarticulate message on the mobile. That moment of 'making room' is what I as a religious person have to notice. It isn't 'pious', it isn't language about God; it's simply language that brings into the world something other than self-defensiveness. It's a breathing space in the asthmatic climate of self-concern and competition; a breathing space that religious language doesn't often manage to create by or for itself.[2]

He goes on to argue that 'Ultimately, the importance of these "secular" words has to stand as a challenge to anything comfortingly religious that we might be tempted to say. This is what human beings *can* find to say in the face of death, religion or no religion. This is what truly makes breathing space for others.'[3]

Rowan Williams' reflections open up an important question: which is the *most religious*, the compassionately secular or the murderously spiritual – an ideology which spawns hatred, or the simple love of one human being for another? Our predominant thought forms often encourage us to divide the world into two: the religious and the non-religious; the sacred and the secular. But I believe that Rowan Williams' thoughts on 11 September and my own reflections in this book on human wellbeing demonstrate the inadequacies of such a duality. These two categories provide a poor structure for making sense of the variegated religious and spiritual universe that surrounds us today. In the fragmented whirl of frenzied communication and constant change against which most of us live, 'the sacred' has become dispersed. We have to learn to look at it differently. We have to learn to look for it differently.

In this concluding section I want to offer a broad-brush analysis of the contemporary territory of religion and spirituality, then to make suggestions as to what Christianity brings to it, particularly in relation to human wellbeing. If secular agencies – and faith communities, for that matter – are to get to grips with the spiritual needs of the population, they need to get to grips with the complexity of this religious and spiritual landscape. We have begun to get used to religious pluralism – to the fact that the Christian tradition is not the only world faith to command a following in our society and to play a role within British culture. But the complexity to which I refer is about more than this. It is about the diverse *ways of being religious* which abound in our society. Exploring this means cutting the cake in a different way. For the issues at stake are – to use contemporary political jargon – cross-cutting ones. That is, these various ways of expressing a religious sensibility can be found in all faith traditions and in none.

In allegorical terms, the parable of Miracle provides insight into our socio-cultural reality. For it is incontrovertible that we live in a society which has lost its simple corporate Christian faith (if it ever had one to lose). The grand narrative of Christianity has faded, though we find its echoes everywhere – from the way we structure our working week to the way we run our criminal justice system. Its normative value systems are still powerful, but we live now amid a rich collection of fragments of faith – of partial languages and limited visions. There is no going back. There is no garden of Eden waiting to be restored; no palace to be reinhabited. On the whole in our society, when it comes to the crunch, we believe in the limitations of material things and we recognize the need to be lifted out of ourselves and beyond ourselves. To say that secularization has made religion less important in our social context is, I think, a mistake. It has made the specificity of Christianity, and its claim upon the majority, less important – but that is different. All the evidence is that as a society we believe in sacred things, in spiritual things. But we name them differently now. As explored already in this book, the challenge for Christians in this context is how to translate ourselves in order to speak meaningfully. We need to recognize that those outside our tradition find our language and concepts baffling. This is not to say that because theological ideas cannot be understood by all of the people all of the time, they should not and cannot be deployed by some of the people some of the time. Quite the opposite, in fact. Those who are schooled and rooted, in detail and in depth, in one particular tradition are a gift. They are our faith-linguists. But if they are to have an impact beyond the boundaries of their faith tradition, they need to get out more and speak more than one language. Only then will theological thoughts and concepts give texture and richness to the body politic.

Miracle was brought up with religion. It shaped her self-identity and imagination, her appreciation of life and love, of beauty and possibility. Many individuals in our society have that experience, but many more do not. Of those who do, some remain closely involved in their faith tradition while others appear to leave it behind. What the story of Miracle shows, however, is that it is not easy to leave behind the shapes and thought forms, values and religious imagination that have been inculcated from birth. To try to do so is like trying to unlearn a language. The only way to do that is to refuse to use it. Even then, memory and the subconscious will have the last word.

Some leave behind their faith traditions while retaining a loyalty to the cultural aspects of religion. This is most noticeable among minority communities and those that face discrimination. So, for instance, it is common to hear people refer to themselves as 'secular Jews' or 'non-practising Muslims', or 'lapsed Catholics'. Here it is clear that religion is still key to the overall jigsaw of human identity, even if religious practice and belief are not prominent aspects of such people's lifestyles. The religious component of human identity in such cases is likely to be revisited at times of individual life-crisis, or when political strife threatens the cultural integrity of communities, or when experiences of discrimination are heightened. For instance, the Muslim identity of a colleague of mine became much more obvious in the wake of the 11 September attacks than it was before them. The increase in racist attacks in the part of town where he lived made that solidarity a necessity.

Among those who remain closely involved with their cradle faith identities, a huge range of religious expression can be observed. Meaning and fulfilment are found in very different ways. For some the most important thing is to have a systematic and easily understandable set of beliefs to which they can assent without question. They usually commit to a concomitant set of ethical values. For others this is the opposite of what they consider religion to be about. They prefer to focus upon the ritual practices which give structure to life and speak of the importance of mystery and questioning rather than of simple answers. For some the communal aspect of faith is what matters – being part of a mutually supportive group. For others this is anathema – they simply want to pray and worship God one-to-one, or practise meditation in private. Some believe in the inextricability of faith and 'the world' – work, politics, leisure; others see religious practice as an escape from the rest of life.

And what of those not born into any kind of faith tradition? How do they fit into the religious and spiritual landscape that we have begun to describe? Some maintain an indifference to things religious throughout life – even unto death. Of these, some are robustly materialist and rationalistic, refusing to countenance any reality beyond the empirically verifiable. Others, however, partake of – even seek out – experiences of transcendence (though they probably wouldn't name them in that way) in so-called non-religious ways. The self-transcendence of play and of love are particularly important in our society: experienced through family and personal relationships, sport, artistic endeavour, movies and music. Some of those with no religious background are endlessly fascinated by religion but feel unable to 'enter into' its thought, forms and culture, much as they may yearn to.

Others are able to make a 'fideistic leap' and convert whole-heartedly to a faith tradition and become part of the life of a committed community despite their lack of religious back-ground. Still others take a pick-and-mix approach to a range of spiritual and religious world-views, a methodology which is despised, often unfairly, by those rooted in a single faith tradition.

This brief sketch of the many and varied ways of being religious and relating to things religious is by no means comprehensive, but it is a start. We can see that understanding spiritual needs is not simply about getting our collective heads around the teachings and lifestyles of a range of world faiths – it is also about an appreciation of the diverse mix of acceptance and rejection, familiarity with and alienation from these faiths. Meeting spiritual needs demands a recognition that individual interpretations of faith traditions are infinitely variable, and the number of spiritual belief systems 'out there' is infinite too.

For those with a practical and professional responsibility for meeting spiritual needs – e.g. as providers of health and social care – the picture that I paint may seem intimidating and complicated. But in my experience this terrain is already pretty daunting. Training in spiritual needs in health care settings, for example, tends to focus upon stereotyped, lowest-common-denominator assumptions about various faiths and cultures. Meeting spiritual needs seems to demand the ability to memorize endlessly-variable shopping lists of requirements which, in the end, may bear no resemblance to the lived reality of those cultures anyhow. A certain amount of such learning is necessary and important: awareness of, for example, how to treat the Koran, what those of the Jewish, Muslim or Hindu faith will and will not eat and drink, and how they treat the bodies of those who have died. Such basic knowledge is crucial for sensitive delivery of services. But in itself this does not equate to 'meeting spiritual needs'. Indeed, if it leads to inaccurate assumptions being made, it may even be counter-productive.

An example will probably help. Imagine a young woman

admitted to hospital with acute mental health needs. It is known that she has a Roman Catholic background. The question is, what does that *mean* in terms of her spiritual needs? Those caring for her may have been taught a range of things about the Catholic faith. They may assume that 'Catholics like to eat fish on Fridays' or 'Catholics take Mass every week' or 'Catholics will want to see a priest'. Such assumptions may help them to care for her, but it is just as likely that they may disastrously undermine her care. For what if this woman, having been brought up a Catholic, now rejects the church because she was abused in childhood by her priest? Suddenly her spiritual needs look very different. Successful treatment of this woman will be impossible without knowledge of and familiarity with Catholic belief systems in general terms. Of greater importance, however, will be her interpretation of these systems as they apply to herself. If, for example, the priest told her that she was responsible for his abuse of her (a common phenomenon), then despite her alienation from her faith, she may well still believe him. 'Neutral' secular logic will be unlikely to have much purchase on her religiously-induced guilt. Meeting her spiritual needs will involve taking her belief systems seriously, getting inside her world-view and her logic.

We can see from this example that 'meeting spiritual needs' demands skills of empathy and communication – and, alongside these, the development of what we might call a religious imagination: entering into people's world-views and understanding how they hang together. Though knowledge and information about a range of faith traditions can help provide a useful foundation, they are no substitute for the deployment of such imagination.

This complex spiritual and religious scene, then, is the reality within which the interface between society and church is played out. This book has focused upon wellbeing as a case study of this interaction. Our concluding task is an assessment of the meaning of human wellbeing as it functions in our society now, and of Christianity's potential to speak of it and to it in a relevant, meaningful and imaginative way. Where is wellbeing to be found? Do concepts of 'God' have any meaning in this search? Is wellbeing to be found in 'delicious disruption' or 'life-giving stability' – do we experience it when things change or when things stay the same? Is it the result of enough or of excess? Is it brought about by accident or design? Is it an end in itself or a by-product of something else?

Those who enjoy neat definitions of concepts will no doubt be frustrated by this stage. I can hear them saying, 'This is all very interesting, but when is she *actually going to define* "wellbeing" and "health" and the difference between them?' I have deliberately avoided doing this so far in order to keep our discussions broad. In my experience, premature closure about exactly what is embraced by a concept can mean that vital bits of the jigsaw-of-meaning are ruled out of discussions at too early a stage. But now is the time to offer some analysis of how the concept of wellbeing is circulating in our society, as a precursor to our concluding theological postscript about possible Christian purchase upon it.

Though I have used words like 'agenda' and 'debate' when referring to health and wellbeing, I am conscious that, when it comes to wellbeing at least, these words are probably too strong. 'Health' is another matter. Over fifty years of the existence of the 'National Health Service' means that there are well-drawn battle-lines regarding political debates about public and private health, preventive and curative health, acute and community health, health management and health delivery, and medical and social models of health (to name but a few). There is clearly both a health agenda in our society and several ongoing health debates. But discussions of wellbeing are more nebulous. They include all of the discussions about health, but also go far beyond them.

This was brought home to me by the contents of a document which passed across my desk as I prepared to write this conclusion. The paper was a review of the work of one of the emerging Local Strategic Partnerships to which I relate as part of my job (see my introduction). Included in it was the proposal that the several categories of work encompassed by the Partnership (e.g. health and wellbeing, lifelong learning, environment, economic development, community safety, social inclusion) should be replaced by three broader headings. These were listed as economic wellbeing, community wellbeing and environmental wellbeing. Seeing 'wellbeing' used in this way enables me to draw two conclusions about it. First, that it is currently functioning not so much as a concept with content, as a space to be filled. It is a live and highly contested space, and one which is very much in its infancy in contemporary politics. Because of this, we are not in a position to talk yet about what it *does* mean, so much as to suggest what it *might* mean.

Second, a preliminary analysis of its emergent meanings reveals that it is being used to articulate and encompass all those things, many of which are indefinable, which 'make people feel better' or 'make life better for people'. More specifically, there is a hint that what is at stake are issues of balance and choice. The hidden message in choosing three 'wellbeing' headings to encompass the work of a Local Strategic Partnership is that community wellbeing can only be found in balancing out the demands of each of these three categories. If the demands of any one of the three – the environment, the economy, or local community need – were to be valued above the other two then this would be to the detriment of the bigger picture that is human wellbeing. In this sense, the popularity of the concept is perhaps unsurprising in a political context where joined-up thinking is highly prized. The parallels for individuals are obvious. According to this emergent definition, human wellbeing is the by-product of a balanced life: work and leisure, love and loss, exercise and inactivity, restraint and indulgence, etc. This understanding of wellbeing shifts our focus from *content* which may look banal or self-evident (e.g. the aim of Local Strategic Partnerships tends to run along the lines, 'to make life better for the people of X'), to the *process* by which such aims are brought about – that is, the tricky political process of balancing conflicting demands in a context of limited resources. The parallel choices facing individuals are no less difficult and demanding.

My first conclusion above – that wellbeing is currently best summed up as a contested space – opens up the possibility of Christian theological engagement in shaping that space. I believe that now is a crucial time to be involved in this way, before meanings become congealed. And if we can contribute with religious imagination and through translatable concepts, then the Christian tradition has many deep and fruitful insights to offer in this task. I end this book with my attempt to articulate, if only briefly, what these might be.

Christianity and wellbeing

Discussions so far in this book have led us to draw certain conclusions about where Christianity must stand in terms of the 'health' component of wellbeing. For instance, we have suggested that Christianity must resist the assumptions and values predominant in global capitalism in order to work for a countercultural vision of health. This is not health as a commodity, squeaky-clean, hygienic and individualistic, but artistic health, visionary health – messy health. This is the kind of health that recognizes the world as it is; a world where 'shit happens', to anyone and to everyone. Natural shit happens randomly, and person-made shit happens both randomly and by design. This should be theology's starting point. Injustice is where shit is spread unjustly and unevenly, either unwittingly or by deliberate policy, so that those with less power get more of it than those with more. In facing up to such injustice, Christianity is redolent with prophetic insight to enable courageous challenge and tireless action.

Perhaps the most useful resource that the Christian tradition brings to a world where 'shit happens' is a framework for incorporating that shit into life so that it enhances human wellbeing rather than undermining it. I have reflected on this at length in earlier chapters. But it is worth repeating that I am not referring here to Christian apologetics, or complex theological explanations for human pain and suffering such as those generated by the many and varied theodicies on the market. In fact, this is the very opposite of what I mean, for such theodicies seem to me, for the most part, to be complex ways of denying the undeniable fact that random shit happens, and that is that. Theodicies are often simply ways of enabling theologians to square various abstract theological circles in defiance of lived reality.

The frameworks I am thinking of are largely symbolic and relational ones. Mary Douglas' sociological analysis of religious ritual, for instance, makes clear that 'Ritual recognizes the potency of disorder,'[4] and that 'religions often sacralise the very unclean things which have been rejected with abhorrence ... dirt, which is normally destructive, sometimes becomes creative.'[5] So the act of drinking the blood of Christ and eating his body, as enacted in the Christian Eucharist, is symbolic of the ongoing hope that life can emerge from death, and positive insight can emerge from otherwise bad experiences. One correspondent wrote to me:

> When people ask me how I am I often reply something like this: 'I am well and I continue to live with pain ... I trust that there is wellbeing and also health, but I live with pain that emerges from spreading degeneration within my spine.' As you know, I see what I have not seen before and discover what I may never have known before!

While capitalist, commodified health would have us invest in the impossible – that death, sickness and old age will never happen to us – a Christian perspective makes us face facts: death and sickness are part of life and wellbeing. As Douglas puts it, 'a garden is not a tapestry; if all the weeds are removed, the soil is impoverished. Somehow the gardener must preserve fertility by returning what he has taken out.' Thus she shows how religions can have transformative powers by providing a language to articulate the hope that bad things can be made powerful for good, 'like turning weeds and lawn cuttings into compost'.[6]

But it is not only through ritual that such incorporation of challenging and negative experiences can happen. It is also a function of the corporate and communal nature of the

Christian faith. As explored in earlier parts of this book, the whole point of Christianity is that it is 'a story-formed community'. Individual wisdom feeds communal wisdom, which in turn enhances individual wisdom in a never-ending cycle. Individual reflections upon personal challenges and limitations are therefore invaluable to the wellbeing of the whole. At its best, the Christian community can provide spaces where such experiences can be shared, both within its boundaries and beyond them. For instance, the following words from Jo Ind about living with multiple sclerosis have inspired and helped many who live with illness and disability, and have challenged many who as yet do not:

> Yes, my condition is a very challenging one to live with, but it is no different from yours. What I am grappling with is not Multiple Sclerosis, it is the human condition. I don't know what the future holds – but neither do you. I don't know what is essentially me, but neither do you. I am not in control of my body, but neither are you. The difference, now I have MS, is that it is less easy than it was to delude myself otherwise. This is a new exciting country, and I am exploring it right where I am.[7]

In an earlier chapter we established that one of the most important attractions of spirituality is that it gives meaning and purpose to life. Insofar as the Christian story can offer structures of meaning, it therefore has the potential to contribute to human wellbeing. However, it is important to distinguish between the construction of meaning and the imposition of explanations. The temptation to explain away sickness, death and loss is ever present, particularly for religious people. It is important, in the face of traumatic life experiences, to hold on to the value of mystery. Crass explanations can undermine human wellbeing, while embracing mystery can enhance it. Those who claim that spirituality is important to them often say that they feel there is something 'out there', in and beyond the world. This dimension can never be fully understood or known, they say, but it somehow makes the world more than the sum of its parts. Some people call this thing 'God', and may venture to say all sorts of systematically worked-out stuff about that God. Others prefer simply to believe in the possibility of intangible and immeasurable things. Living with such mystery means that outcomes can never be entirely predictable. It means believing in the possibility that human beings may be moved to do truly miraculous and surprising things. It means working to develop, in Rowan Williams' words, 'a language that brings into the world something other than self-defensiveness . . . breathing space(s) in the asthmatic climate of self-concern and competition'.[8]

To believe in mystery is to believe in miracles. Miracles happen all the time, if we look in the right places. I'm not referring, of course, to supernatural divine interventions. Such things may happen – who am I to deny the possibility? But if they never have, this takes nothing away from the possibility of miracles. I refer instead to the startling transformations that happen all the time in our society, sometimes in apparently small ways. For instance, when a victim of sexual abuse is enabled to take the first steps towards becoming a survivor because someone to whom she tells her story actually believes her; when a young person turns away from persistent offending because he finds a youth support worker who isn't scared of him and understands what is really going on; when a young woman decides against suicide because a new relationship suddenly makes her life worth living. These are miraculous happenings.

Miracles lie in the fact that despite its fragility, human life is also amazingly resilient, tenacious and adaptable. Yes, we can be annihilated in an instant. But we can also survive against incredible odds, and transform the dreadful into the beautiful. I hope this Christian truth, at least, is readily translatable: shit happens – but in the face of it, human wellbeing is a possibility. This is the stuff of love, mystery and miracles.

NOTES

Introduction

1 A. R. Webster, *Found Wanting: Women, Christianity and Sexuality*, London: Cassell, 1995.

2 H. Orchard, 'Health Care Contexts – Spiritual Care Debates' in H. Orchard (ed.), *Spirituality in Health Care Contexts*, London: Westminster John Knox Press, 2001, 9–18, p. 9.

3 S. Pattison, 'Public Theology: A Polemical Epilogue', *Political Theology*, 2 (2000), 57–76, p. 57.

4 Pattison, 'Public Theology', p. 57.

5 Pattison, 'Public Theology', p. 72.

6 D. W. Hardy, *Finding the Church*, London: SCM Press, 2000, p.110.

Chapter 1: Well?

1 D. Haraway, 'A Cyborg Manifesto: Science, Technology, and Socialist-Feminism in the Late Twentieth Century' in D. Haraway, *Simians, Cyborgs, and Women: The Reinvention of Nature*, London: Free Association Books, 1991, 149–181, p. 150.

2 Haraway, 'A Cyborg Manifesto', p. 152.

3 Haraway, 'A Cyborg Manifesto', p. 151.

4 M. Wilson, *Health is for People*, London: Darton, Longman & Todd, 1976, p. 61.

5 C. Marrs, 'Globalization: A Short Introduction', *Political Theology*, forthcoming.

6 J. Winterson, *Art Objects: Essays on Ecstasy and Effrontery*, London: Vintage, 1996, p. 135.

7 Winterson, *Art Objects*, p. 138.

8 Winterson, *Art Objects*, p. 135.

9   Winterson, *Art Objects*, p. 136.

10 Winterson, *Art Objects*, p. 138.

11 Winterson, *Art Objects*, p. 139.

12 A. Solomon, *The Noonday Demon: An Anatomy of Depression*, London: Chatto & Windus, 2001, p. 32.

13 Wilson, *Health is for People*, p. 31.

14 J. Ind, *Fat is a Spiritual Issue: My Journey*, London: Mowbray, 1993, p. 1.

15 Ind, *Fat is a Spiritual Issue*, p. 5.

16 Ind, *Fat is a Spiritual Issue*, p. 57.

17 Ind, *Fat is a Spiritual Issue*, p. 48.

18 Ind, *Fat is a Spiritual Issue*, p. 49.

19 E. Hoffman, *Lost in Translation*, London: Minerva, 1989, pp. 51–2.

20 Wilson, *Health is for People*, p. 2.

21 Wilson, *Health is for People*, p. 55.

22 A. Wright, *Why Bother with Theology?*, London: Darton, Longman & Todd, 2002, p. 39.

23 Wright, *Why Bother with Theology?*, p. 42.

24 Haraway, 'A Cyborg Manifesto', p. 153.

25 Haraway, 'A Cyborg Manifesto', p. 174.

26 Haraway, 'A Cyborg Manifesto', p. 154.

27 Haraway, 'A Cyborg Manifesto', p. 180.

28 Haraway, 'A Cyborg Manifesto', p. 150.

29 Haraway, 'A Cyborg Manifesto', p. 154.

30 Solomon, *The Noonday Demon*, p. 32.

Chapter 2: Sick?

1   J. Kristeva, *Powers of Horror: An Essay on Abjection*, New York: Columbia University Press, 1982, p. 4.

2   M. Douglas, *Purity and Danger*, London: Ark Paperbacks, 1984.

3   M. Wilson, *Health is for People*, London: Darton, Longman & Todd, 1976, p. 67.

4   Thanks to Mary Beasley of Birmingham for an email correspondence in which she put forward these thoughts on scapegoating.

5   K. Duff, *The Alchemy of Illness*, London: Virago, 1994, p.115.

6   Kristeva, *Powers of Horror*, p. 3.

7 Wilson, *Health is for People*, p. 29.

8 G. Rose, *Love's Work*, London: Chatto & Windus, 1995, p. 73.

9 S. Sontag, *Illness As Metaphor*, London: Penguin, 1977, pp. 11–12.

10 Duff, *The Alchemy of Illness*, p.39.

11 Duff, *The Alchemy of Illness*, p. 38.

12 S. Sontag, *AIDS and its Metaphors*, London: Penguin, 1988, p. 38.

13 Sontag, *AIDS and its Metaphors*, p. 38–9.

14 L. Brooks, *Guardian*, G2, 20 March 2002, p. 4.

15 P. Lennon, *Guardian*, G2, 20 March 2002, p. 15.

16 Duff, *The Alchemy of Illness*, p. 5.

17 Sontag, *Illness As Metaphor*, pp. 9–10.

18 Duff, *The Alchemy of Illness*, p. 115.

19 Sontag, *Illness As Metaphor*, p. 51.

20 Sontag, *Illness As Metaphor*, p. 53.

21 Sontag, *Illness As Metaphor*, p. 58.

22 Sontag, *Illness As Metaphor*, p. 59.

23 Duff, *The Alchemy of Illness*, p. 41.

24 Duff, *The Alchemy of Illness*, p. 30.

25 A. Solomon, *The Noonday Demon: An Anatomy of Depression*, London: Chatto & Windus, 2001, p. 20–1.

26 *Promoting Mental Health: The Role of Faith Communities – Jewish and Christian Perspectives*, London: Health Education Authority, 1999, p. 5.

27 N. Sagovsky, 'A Dialogue on Personality Disorders: A Theologian's Questions' in *Personality Disorder and Human Worth*, papers from a conference organized by the Board for Social Responsibility, London: Church of England, 2001, 31–42, pp. 33, 36.

28 B. Johnson, 'Modern Day Lepers' in *Personality Disorder and Human Worth*, 13–20, p. 14.

29 Johnson, 'Modern Day Lepers', p. 17.

30 Duff, *The Alchemy of Illness*, p. 11.

31 Duff, *The Alchemy of Illness*, p. 37.

32 Sontag, *Illness As Metaphor*, p. 62.

33 Duff, *The Alchemy of Illness*, p. 35.

34 Sontag, *Illness As Metaphor*, p. 85.

35 Sontag, *Illness As Metaphor*, p. 87.

36 Douglas, *Purity and Danger*, pp. 161, 162.

37 Duff, *The Alchemy of Illness*, p. 103.

38 Duff, *The Alchemy of Illness*, p. 9.

39 Quoted Duff, *The Alchemy of Illness*, p. 56.

40 Solomon, *The Noonday Demon*, p. 19.

41 Solomon, *The Noonday Demon*, p. 24.

42 J. Ind, *Fat is a Spiritual Issue: My Journey*, London: Mowbray, 1993, pp. 105–6.

43 Duff, *The Alchemy of Illness*, p. 83.

44 Duff, *The Alchemy of Illness*, p. 33.

45 See, for example, R. Picardie, *Before I Say Goodbye*, London: Penguin, 1998; J. Diamond, *C: Because Cowards Get Cancer Too*, London: Vermillion, 1998, p. 5.

46 M. Davies and A. Webster, *The Dying Game: A Young Person's Guide to Death*, Birmingham: Student Christian Movement Publications, 1997, p. 5.

47 Duff, *The Alchemy of Illness*, pp. 41–2.

48 Duff, *The Alchemy of Illness*, p. 43.

Chapter 3: Healing?

1 W. H. Vanstone, *The Stature of Waiting*, London: Darton, Longman & Todd, 1982.

2 Vanstone, *The Stature of Waiting*, p. 46.

3 Vanstone, *The Stature of Waiting*, p. 35.

4 Vanstone, *The Stature of Waiting*, p. 65.

5 Vanstone, *The Stature of Waiting*, p. 75.

6 Vanstone, *The Stature of Waiting*, p. 94.

7 Vanstone, *The Stature of Waiting*, p. 96.

8 Vanstone, *The Stature of Waiting*, p. 109.

9 K. Duff, *The Alchemy of Illness*, London: Virago, 1994, p. 33.

10 Duff, *The Alchemy of Illness*, pp. 41–2.

11 Vanstone, *The Stature of Waiting*, p. 113.

12 A. Webster, 'Good News for the Socially Excluded? Blairism, Globalization and the Future of Welfare: Response to Professor Elaine Graham', *Political Theology*, 2 (2000), 100–6.

13 Webster, 'Good News for the Socially Excluded?' p. 102.

14 Duff, *The Alchemy of Illness*, p. 83.

15 I. R. Petrie, *Unleashing the Lion: Towards a Pastoral Theology of Health and Healing*, London: SPCK, 2000, p. 184.

16 E. Dowler, A. Blair, A. Donkin, D. Rex, C. Grundy, *Measuring Access to Healthy Food in Sandwell*, Final Report, published by the University of Warwick and the Sandwell Health Action Zone, June 2001, p. 36.

17 M. Howard et al., *Poverty: The Facts*, fourth edition, London: Child Poverty Action Group, 2001, p. 117.

18 Howard et al., *Poverty*, p. 116.

19 *The Health of Men in Worcestershire: the basis for a strategy to promote the health of men – a document to discuss, dissect and develop*, Worcester: Directorate of Public Health, Worcestershire Health Authority, September 1999.

20 *A Proposal for a Durham Centre for Prison Health Research and Development*, Report of a Working Group of Interested Parties in Durham (January 2001), p. 6.

21 *The Health of Men in Worcestershire*, p. 1.

22 *The Health of Men in Worcestershire*, p. 2.

23 S. Arora, N. Coker, S. Gillam, H. Ismail, *Improving the Health of Black and Minority Ethnic Groups: A Guide for PCGs*, London: King's Fund, 2000, p. 1.

24 Arora et al., *Improving the Health of Black and Minority Ethnic Groups*, pp. 16–17.

25 Hansard, 9 November 2001.

26 Comments made at the conference 'Just as Well' (May 2000), organized jointly by Worcestershire Health Authority and the Church of England Board for Social Responsibility in the Diocese of Worcester.

27 J. Ind, *Fat is a Spiritual Issue: My Journey*, London: Mowbray, 1993, pp. 54–5.

28 A. James, 'Speaking Out', *Guardian*, G2, 9 January 2002, p. 6.

29 J. Tew, 'Getting Social: Championing a Holistic Model of Mental Distress within Professional Education', *Social Work Education*, Vol. 21(2), April 2002.

30 Vanstone, *The Stature of Waiting*, p. 96.

31 J. and J. Austen, 'Disability and Discipleship', *British Journal of Theological Education*, Vol. 8, No. 2 (Summer 1996), 10–15, pp. 10–11.

32 Duff, *The Alchemy of Illness*, p. 11.

33 A. Solomon, *The Noonday Demon: An Anatomy of Depression*, London: Chatto & Windus, 2001, p. 132.

34 J. Swinton and S. Pattison, 'Come all ye faithful', *Health Service*

Journal, Thursday 20 December 2001, 24–5, p. 24.

35 L. Friedli, 'Social and Spiritual Capital: Building "Emotional Resilience" in Communities and Individuals', *Political Theology*, 4 (2001), 55–64, p. 61.

36 J. Kristeva, *Powers of Horror: An Essay on Abjection*, New York: Columbia University Press, 1982, p. 208.

37 Solomon, *The Noonday Demon*, p. 19.

38 G. Rose, *Love's Work*, London: Chatto & Windus, 1995, p. 96.

39 M. Wilson, *Health is for People*, London: Darton, Longman & Todd, 1976, p. 118.

40 M. Duggan with A. Cooper and J. Foster, 'Modernising the Social Model in Mental Health: A Discussion Paper', Social Perspectives Network for Mental Health, 2002, p. 2.

41 T. Jowell, Minister of State for Public Health, Foreword to *Perspectives in Public Health*, ed. S. Griffiths and D. J. Hunter, Abingdon: Radcliffe Medical Press, 1999, p. viii.

42 L. Friedli, 'Social and Spiritual Capital: Building "Emotional Resilience" in Communities and Individuals', pp. 58–9.

43 Solomon, *The Noonday Demon*, p. 131.

44 Duggan with A. Cooper and J. Foster, 'Modernising the Social Model in Mental Health', p. 14.

45 *On Your Doorstep: Community Organisations and Mental Health*, London: Sainsbury Centre for Mental Health, 2000.

46 Swinton and Pattison, 'Come all ye faithful', p. 24.

47 J. Neuberger, Foreword in H. Orchard (ed.), *Spirituality in Health Care Contexts*, London: Westminster John Knox Press, 2001, p. 7.

48 D. Lyall, 'Spiritual Institutions' in Orchard (ed.), *Spirituality in Health Care Contexts*, p. 49.

49 Swinton and Pattison, 'Come all ye faithful', p. 24.

50 S. Pattison, 'Dumbing Down the Spirit' in H. Orchard, (ed.), *Spirituality in Health Care Contexts*, p. 37.

51 H. Orchard and D. Clark, 'Soul Survivors', *Health Service Journal*, 23 August 2001, 28–9.

52 Orchard and Clark, 'Soul Survivors', p. 28.

53 Orchard and Clark, 'Soul Survivors', pp. 28–9.

54 Orchard and Clark, 'Soul Survivors', p. 29.

55 Orchard and Clark, 'Soul Survivors', p. 29.

56 Orchard and Clark, 'Soul Survivors', p. 29.

57 Swinton and Pattison, 'Come all ye faithful', p. 25.

58 Pattison, 'Dumbing Down the Spirit', p. 38.

59 D. W. Hardy, *Finding the Church*, London: SCM Press, 2000, p. 95.

60 Orchard (ed.), *Spirituality in Health Care Contexts*.

61 D. Lyall, 'Spiritual Institutions' in Orchard (ed.), *Spirituality in Health Care Contexts*, pp. 50–1.

62 Pattison, 'Dumbing Down the Spirit', p. 34.

63 N. Copsey, *Forward in Faith: An Experiment in Building Bridges between Ethnic Communities and Mental Health Services in East London*, London: Sainsbury Centre for Mental Health, 2001, p. 10.

64 Copsey, *Forward in Faith*, p. 7.

65 Copsey, *Forward in Faith*, p. 13.

66 Copsey, *Forward in Faith*, p. 15.

67 Pattison, 'Dumbing Down the Spirit', p. 33.

68 Lyall, 'Spiritual Institutions', p. 54.

69 Pattison, 'Dumbing Down the Spirit', p. 35.

70 J. Winterson, *Art Objects: Essays on Ecstasy and Effrontery*, London: Vintage, 1996, p. 146.

71 E. Hoffman, *Lost in Translation*, London: Minerva, 1989, p. 209.

72 Hoffman, *Lost in Translation*, p. 211.

73 Hoffman, *Lost in Translation*, p. 273.

74 Hoffman, *Lost in Translation*, p. 273.

Chapter 4: Miracles?

1 R. Williams, *Writing in the Dust: Reflections on 11th September and its Aftermath*, London: Hodder & Stoughton, 2002, p. 13.

2 Williams, *Writing in the Dust*, pp. 4–5.

3 Williams, *Writing in the Dust*, p. 12.

4 M. Douglas, *Purity and Danger*, London: Ark Paperbacks, 1984, p. 94.

5 Douglas, *Purity and Danger*, p. 159.

6 Douglas, *Purity and Danger*, p. 163.

7 J. Ind, 'Finding My Bearings in a Strange Country – Multiple Sclerosis', *Third Way*, Vol. 23, No. 2. (March 2000), Harrow: Third Way Trust Ltd.

8 Williams, *Writing in the Dust*, p. 5.

INDEX